D1503475

WOMEN WORKING IT OUT

Career Plans and Business Decisions

Julianne Nelson

University Press of America,® Inc.
Lanham · New York · Oxford

Copyright © 2003 by
University Press of America,® Inc.
4720 Boston Way
Lanham, Maryland 20706

PO Box 317
Oxford
OX2 9RU, UK

ISBN 0-7618-2493-6 (paperback : alk. ppr.)

*This book is dedicated to the memory of my
parents, Vilmer and Harriet Nelson.*

TABLE OF CONTENTS:

LIST OF TABLES:

Preface

Much of my career has been spent teaching microeconomics to undergraduates, graduate students and business professionals. In the process, I have been forced to admit that economists (myself included) often have a hard time making concepts like marginal revenue and opportunity cost *feel* genuinely useful. The typical introductory text (or lecture) tends to use bland generic examples to illustrate the economic principles of interest. It is left to the reader (or listener) to figure out how to use these principles in daily life.

This book represents my attempt to fill part of this void. As the title suggests, the book is primarily intended for women -- particularly those facing mid-life career decisions. Nevertheless, the examples presented in the text are appropriate for *anyone* wanting to learn how to use economic principles to solve familiar business and professional problems.

In general, I hope to encourage my readers to think more creatively about how they "allocate" their time. As we all know, there are only so many hours in the day. This means that our time is a scarce and *valuable* resource, one to be spent judiciously. I believe that the core economic principles of opportunity cost and marginal analysis provide useful guidance as we confront this ubiquitous question. The examples in this book are intended to show how to put this belief into practice. It is, of course, up to you to decide whether this approach is any more helpful than the standard textbook treatment of this material.

This work would not have been possible without the enthusiastic support of Rita Simon and her Women's Freedom Network (a non-profit organization that Rita founded several years ago). My deepest thanks to a wonderful friend! I would also like to express my gratitude to the friends and colleagues who provided encouragement and advice along the way. I am particularly grateful to Debbie Lamb-Mechanick and Kay House, two very important people in my life who read numerous drafts of the manuscript and shared their opinions on everything from the realism of my examples to the appropriateness of my word choices and my spelling. The book would not be the same without them!

As ever, I must take credit for any glitches that remain. If you find any, please just consider them as evidence to support my favorite unproveable theorem: "There is *always* at least one typographical error in any manuscript."

※ ※ ※

An Invitation
to Consider

Are you thinking about changing jobs? going into business for yourself? re-entering the workforce? retiring and starting a new career? taking on a new part-time job? starting over after being laid-off or going through a divorce? If so, then this book is for you. It is designed to help you refine your business intuition by showing you how to use economic and financial principles to make career decisions.

After working through the examples in this book, you will have seen how to identify your options in terms of their benefits and costs – and how to make decisions on the basis of your analysis. Although business principles such as *opportunity cost* and *marginal analysis* do not magically resolve all questions, they *can* help you clarify the issues involved in making business decisions – and ultimately help you choose the option that works best for you both financially and personally.

Most of the examples in this book reflect the day-to-day reality of an independent contractor or the owner of a small business. The scenarios range from a look at the decisions faced by sole proprietors working alone to a discussion of the issues confronting retail store operators, small-scale craft manufacturers and the owner/managers of for-profit companies providing professional services such as accounting, health care or management consulting. These cases were chosen to illustrate the variety of options available to women considering career changes. They are designed to be as realistic as possible, with actual price and cost data used whenever available. The cases discussed in this book can be readily updated and adapted to suit your individual needs. The general principles presented apply to virtually all business activities, no matter what the product or service or scale of operations.

The common thread that runs throughout these chapters is an emphasis on *the impact of change*. In each situation, we will start by looking at how a new business opportunity is likely to affect the status quo – both pro and con. We will then use this information to identify the best available alternative – the one that produces the greatest benefit for you, the business owner.

We start the next chapter by looking at the financial consequences of leaving your current occupation – whether it be employee, contractor or home-maker. In Chapter 3, we discuss how to extend the analysis to look at the value *to you* of taking a new job or (re)entering the work force.

In later chapters, we assume that you have decided to go ahead and start your own business. With this in mind, we present examples designed to show you how to use economic and financial principles to manage your business to your best advantage. In Chapter 4 you will see how to use the basic notion of opportunity cost to figure out whether or not you can expect to break even on a particular business venture. Chapter 5 shows you how to use marginal analysis to choose the size and scope of your business. Chapter 6 combines these two approaches, using both opportunity cost and marginal analysis to develop pricing strategies for your products and services. In Chapter 7, you will see how to apply this approach to a wider variety of situations – and discover the consequences of ignoring its insights.

By the end of the book, you should be more familiar with the basic logic of these business principles. Ideally, you will come to see these principles as the basis for a practical approach to making *choices* -- whether or not to go into business for yourself, what variety of goods and services to offer, how much to sell, what price to charge, what production methods to use, etc. In short, you will have found a practical guide to asking – and answering – the questions you face as you start to work things out for yourself.

☶ ☶ ☶

2

THE CONSEQUENCES of CHANGING THE STATUS QUO

The question of whether or not to change your job – and your life – has never been easy. In recent years, employer-employee relationships have evolved to make this decision feel even more complicated. People who once were paid an annual salary or who worked full-time for an hourly wage may now be hired on an "as-needed" basis. They may work as independent contractors, or be assigned to several work sites by an employment agency. They might also work on a commission or piece-rate basis, or share a job with a co-worker.

Despite the abundance of new career categories, the initial question for anyone considering a career change remains a simple one: "How much money do I need to earn to maintain my standard of living if I leave my current position?" Maintaining your "standard of living" does not necessarily mean replicating your current income -- it could also mean taking a job you like better and accepting less money (or a job you like less but with higher pay).

For the moment, let's assume that you are considering jobs with working conditions that are similar to the status quo. Specifically, you expect to feel the same way about a new job as you now feel about your current position. (In the next chapter we will tackle the broader question of how to adjust for any changes in lifestyle implied by a new job.)

Given this assumption, you will need to replace your current income and benefits – your current total compensation – in order to maintain your current standard of living. The next step is to find an appropriate measure of your earnings. As you do this, you need to remember that the best measure of your compensation is *not* defined by your salary alone or by what your employer now spends on you. Instead, business principles define the relevant measure of your compensation as the amount you will need to replicate your current base salary or wage *along with* the non-wage benefits your employer currently provides. This dollar amount represents what you are giving up (in financial terms) by leaving your current position. Economists define this to be the *opportunity cost* of your choice to leave.

The essential logic of opportunity costs – the notion of looking at benefits foregone as well as advantages obtained when making a decision – makes it easier to compare the specific strengths and weaknesses of available options and to reach a decision on that basis. The purpose of this chapter is to show you how this theory works in practice. You will first have a chance to see how three women would compute their own opportunity costs. You will then be ready to try the technique out for yourself.

ꭥ ꭥ ꭥ

THE OPPORTUNITY COST OF CHANGE

Once you pose the question of changing the status quo in terms of replacing your current compensation, the financial aspects of the issue become easier to tackle. You are left with the task of figuring out how much you now earn in terms of salary, wages, bonuses, benefits, etc. and then comparing this amount with the other benefits of changing jobs – including quality-of-life issues such as shorter commutes, more job satisfaction, less stress, more time with your family, more autonomy, and even lower dry cleaning bills.

To see how this approach works, let's consider three typical cases.[1] First we have Beverly, an accountant who works for a small public accounting firm and receives an annual salary, along with health and retirement benefits. In the past, she has also been awarded a bonus at the end of each year. Next we have Fran, a Registered Nurse who works at a metropolitan hospital and is paid on an hourly basis. She works one overtime shift each month, and usually receives a wage increase at the end of the year. She receives health benefits, but does not participate in an employer-sponsored retirement plan. Last, we have Sally, a part-time Emergency Medical Technician (EMT) who works weekends and evenings as needed. Her employer pays its share of Social Security and Medicare taxes, but does not provide any other benefits for its part-time workers and rarely gives pay raises.

All of these women are thinking about some sort of career change, but are not sure how it would affect their family finances. At this point, the nature of the new careers being considered does not matter. The first question they much each tackle is "How much do I currently earn?" They will later face the task of evaluating alternatives to the status quo, in terms of both their financial and personal implications.

Beverly: Total Compensation for a Salaried Professional

As a cost accountant in Washington, DC, Beverly currently has a base salary of $63,130 a year, the average for the region. This value gives Beverly the best place to start when figuring her total annual compensation – and the opportunity cost of changing jobs next year. She must next figure out her expected base salary next year and compute what it would cost her to replace the benefits that she currently receives from her employer. After finishing this exercise, Beverly was surprised to discover that her *total* compensation was $77,003, roughly 22 percent higher than her base salary. In other words, Beverly would have to earn 22 percent more than her current base salary in order to replace the full amount she expects to receive from her current job next year. Table 2-1 summarizes her calculations.

Table 2-1: Opportunity Cost for a Salaried Employee

Type of Compensation	Nature of Payment	Value
Base Salary	annual amount	$63,130
Annual Bonus	5% of base salary	$3,157
FICA (employer's share)	6.2% of salary and bonus	$4,110
Medicare (employer's share)	1.45% of salary and bonus	$961
Retirement (employer's contribution)	4% of base salary	$2,525
Health (employer's contribution)	$135 per month	$1,620
Disability Insurance	annual cost of individual policy	$1,500
	TOTAL	**$77,003**

Let's look at the details of her compensation.

Base Salary: Beverly's company has a policy of granting pay raises only when an employee is promoted to a new, more demanding job. Since Beverly is not in line for a promotion at this time, she expects her base pay to remain at its current level next year.

- Beverly expects her base salary to be $63,130 next year.

Annual Bonus: Beverly's company uses a system of annual bonuses to reward superior performance by employees not currently in line for promotion. These bonuses result in one-time cash payments, but do not have an impact on future salaries. Beverly has consistently received favorable performance reviews and has been awarded an annual bonus equal to 5 percent (or

.05) of her base salary in recent years. We can now see how Beverly has estimated her annual bonus for next year.

- Beverly expects a 5 percent annual bonus of .05 x $63,130 = $3,157 next year.

Self-Employment Taxes: Beverly knows that if she decides to work for herself, she will have to pay "self-employment" taxes on her earned income. In other words, she will have to pay *both* the employer and the employee's share of Social Security (FICA) and Medicare taxes. In 2001, the employer's share of FICA taxes was equal to 6.2 percent (or .062) of the first $80,400 of earned income; the employer's share of Medicare taxes was equal to 1.45 percent (or .0145) of all earned income. In Beverly's case, this means that she will have to pay self-employment taxes on both her base salary and her annual bonus.

- Based on her *total* expected "earned income" for next year, Beverly estimates the value of her employer's 6.2 percent FICA contribution to be .062 x ($63,130 + $3,157) = $4,110.

- Substituting .0145 for .062, Beverly estimates the value of her employer's 1.45 percent Medicare contribution to be .0145 x ($63,130 + $3,157) = $961.

Retirement Benefits: Beverly's employer also offers retirement benefits: the firm matches her contributions to a tax-sheltered retirement account on a dollar-for-dollar basis (for up to 5 percent of her *base* salary). Beverly currently transfers 4 percent (or .04) of her base salary to the company-sponsored plan, and the company contributes an equal amount. If she were to go into business for herself, Beverly would be able to deposit money in a similar tax-sheltered plan as a self-employed individual, but she would no longer have the benefit of the matching contributions.

- Beverly expects the value of her employer's 4 percent contributions to her retirement account to be .04 x $63,130 = $2,525.

Insurance Benefits: Beverly and her employer currently split the cost of her health insurance: the company contributes $120 per month and Beverly pays the remainder of the premium. She expects her overall health care premium to be the same next year if she keeps her current job. If Beverly were self-employed, she would be responsible for the full amount of the monthly premium. She also knows that under these circumstances her total health care premium would increase by $15 per month.[2] As a self-employed professional she will no longer qualify for the group rate she now receives through her employer. Beverly's opportunity cost of health benefits includes *both* the cash value of her current employer's subsidy *and* the change in monthly premium attributable to her change in status.

- The value to Beverly of her current health benefits is $120 + $15 = $135 per month.

- The annual value to Beverly of these benefits is $135 x 12 = $1,620.

Beverly's current employer also pays for disability insurance on behalf of all of its employees. Beverly wants to maintain some form of this coverage even if she decides to work for herself. She knows that the cost of this insurance will depend on her self-employment earnings and her personal circumstances.

- Beverly expects to pay $1500 per year for a disability policy similar to the one her employer currently provides.

Unused Benefits: There are other benefits offered by her employer, but they are ones that Beverly does not want or need. For example, the accounting firm automatically purchases term life insurance for all staff. Since her personal circumstances make such insurance unnecessary, this benefit does not represent an opportunity cost to Beverly – even if it *does* represent a cost to her employer.

Summing Up: At this point, Beverly can look more carefully at the financial consequences taking specific new jobs. Table 2-1 gives her a concise summary of her findings; she knows that it will take roughly $77,000 to replicate her current earnings. She is now able to compare this amount with the benefits of available alternatives, both in terms of compensation levels and quality-of-life implications. As we will see in a later section, she can also use this figure to estimate a minimum necessary billing rate as if she decides to work for herself.

KEY POINTS TO REMEMBER:

❑   If you are a salaried employee, your total
     expected compensation consists of
     ▪   your base pay,
     ▪   anticipated merit and/or cost-of-living
          increases,
     ▪   an allowance for self-employment taxes, and
     ▪   the cost that *you* would incur when replacing
          the benefits you now receive.

❑   Self-employment taxes are designed to replace
     the share of Social Security and Medicare taxes
     normally paid by employers.

Fran: Total Compensation for a Full-Time Hourly Worker

As a registered nurse at a hospital in Milwaukee, Wisconsin, Fran currently earns a base wage of $23.04 per hour plus benefits. The task of computing her total compensation is a

little more complicated than it was for Beverly, since Fran has to
account explicitly for holidays, annual leave, and overtime pay.
Table 2-2 summarizes Fran's findings. Like Beverly, she was
surprised to find that her current total compensation – her
opportunity cost of changing jobs – exceeded her base pay by
almost 20 percent.

Table 2-2: Opportunity Cost for a Full-Time Hourly Employee

Type of Compensation	Nature of Payment	Value
Base Wage Rate	$23.50 per hour for 2080 hours per year (includes annual cost-of living increase)	$48,880
Overtime	$35.00 per hour of overtime; 8 hours worked per month	$3,610
FICA (employer's share)	6.2% of salary (including cost-of-living increase)	$3,254
Medicare (employer's share)	1.45% of salary (including cost-of-living increase)	$761
Health insurance	Employer contribution plus cost differential for individual policy	$0
Term Life Insurance	Annual replacement cost	$156
Disability Insurance	Annual replacement cost	$1,600
Professional Dues	Employer subsidy for license fees and conference participation	$250
TOTAL		**$58,511**

Let's consider the details of her earnings.

Hours Paid at Base Wage: Although Fran's base pay is quoted
as an hourly rate, she is a full-time employee with 10 paid
holidays and 13 personal leave days per year. To estimate the
financial consequences of changing jobs, she assumes that there

are exactly 52 weeks in the year, with potentially 5 work days per week. Since a full work day for Fran consists of one 8-hour shift, there are 40 hours in her typical work week.

• As a full-time employee, Fran is paid her base hourly rate for 40 x 52 = 2080 hours per year.

Expected Base Pay: The hospital where Fran works does not offer performance bonuses, but it has recently been granting modest cost-of-living increases. She expects her hourly rate to increase by 2 percent (or .02) next year.

• Fran expects to earn 1.02 x $23.04 = $23.50 per hour next year.

• Fran expects her annual base pay to be $23.50 x 2080 = $48,880 next year.

Overtime Pay: Fran generally works 8 hours of overtime each month – one weekend daytime shift per month. Her contract with the hospital ensures that she is paid time-and-a-half for overtime and an additional 5 percent as a weekend differential. In other words, she earns 155 percent of her base wage for these weekend hours. If she stays at her current job, she expects to continue working one overtime shift per month next year.

• Fran expects to work 8 x 12 = 96 hours of overtime next year if she stays at her current job.

• Fran expects her overtime rate to be 155 percent of her base wage next year, or 1.55 x $23.50 = $37.60 per hour.

• Fran expects to earn 96 x $35 = $3,610 in overtime pay next year if she stays at her current job.

Self-Employment Taxes: Like Beverly, Fran knows that she will
have to pay self-employment taxes on her earned income if she
goes into business for herself.

- Based on her total expected earnings for next year, Fran
  estimates the value of the hospital's FICA contribution
  to be .062 x ($48,880 + $3,610) = $3,254.

- Substituting .0145 for .062, Fran estimates the value of
  her employer's Medicare contribution to be .0145 x
  ($48,880 + $3,610) = $761.

Insurance Benefits: Fran has chosen to opt out of the hospital's
health insurance plan since her husband's employer offers
similar coverage for employee spouses at a lower price. As a
result, the value to Fran of her employer's health insurance
benefits is $0.

Unlike Beverly, Fran feels that life insurance is an important
component of her family's finances. It will cost her $13 per
month to maintain the coverage now provided by her employer.

- The value to Fran of her employer's life insurance
  benefit is $13 x 12 = $156 per year.

Fran also intends to purchase disability coverage if she
decides to work for herself. Given her profession and her
personal circumstances, she knows that it will cost her $1600 per
year to replace the coverage the hospital currently purchases on
her behalf.

Other Benefits: To encourage staff to continue their
professional training, the hospital where Fran works offers to pay
up to $250 per year to cover the cost of professional licenses,
membership in professional organizations, continuing education,
subscriptions to work-related publications, etc. Fran uses this
money to pay her annual dues in several professional nursing

associations, an expense she expects to incur whether or not she continues in her present job.

- The value to Fran of her employer's contribution to professional expenses would be $250 per year as long as she would incur this expense in her next job. (If she intended to let her memberships lapse after leaving the hospital, then the value to her of this benefit would be $0.)

Summing up: After creating Table 2-2, Fran has enough information to evaluate a wide range of alternatives to the status quo. She knows that it will take just over $58,500 to replace the compensation she would earn next year in her current job. She is now better able to decide whether or not it would make sense to switch to an independent contractor status and work at several different hospitals or to change careers entirely.

KEY POINTS TO REMEMBER:

If you are an employee paid on an hourly basis, your total expected compensation typically depends upon

- ❏ hours spent on the job during your regular work week,
- ❏ the number of paid holidays you take,
- ❏ the number of personal leave days you take,
- ❏ shift differentials (if appropriate),
- ❏ overtime hours (if appropriate),
- ❏ self employment taxes and
- ❏ the cost to you of replacing the benefits you now receive.

---

16   Chapter 2: Changing the Status Quo

Sally: Total Compensation for a Part-Time Hourly Worker

As a part-time EMT working with a fire department in Atlanta, Sally earns a base hourly wage of $13.30 per hour, the average for the area. Her hourly rate is higher whenever she works in the evening, at night or on weekends. Although her schedule varies from month to month, Sally knows that she needs to look at an "average" month in order to figure out her opportunity cost of changing jobs. Table 2-3 and Table 2-4 below summarize the results of her analysis.

Shift Differentials: Sally's contract specifies that her hourly rate is 5 percent (.05) higher when she is called to work in the evening and 10 percent (.10) higher when she is called to work at night during the week. If she is called to work a day shift on a weekend, her hourly rate is 17 percent (.17) higher. When Sally works an evening or a night shift on a weekend, she gets *two* differentials: on a weekend evening, she earns an hourly rate that is 22.85 percent (.2285) higher than her base rate; for a weekend night, she earns a rate that is 28.7 percent (.287) higher than her base wage.[34] Given the current financial status of her employer, Sally expects these rates to be the same next year if she stays at her current job. Table 2-3 summarizes these rates.

Table 2-3: Hourly Wage Rates for a Part-Time Worker

Wage Rate	Method of Computation	Value
Base Wage	Hourly rate	$13.30
Evening Differential	5% of base rate	$13.97
Night Differential	10% of base rate	$14.63
Weekend Differential	17% of base rate	$15.56
Weekend Evening Differential	22.85% of base rate	$16.34
Weekend Night Differential	28.7% of base rate	$17.12

Expected Earnings: Although Sally works on an "as-needed" basis, she ends up working roughly the same type and number of

shifts each month.   In a typical month, she will work two
weekend day shifts, one weekend night shift and one regular
night shift during the week.   Although she only works part-time,
she does not have to pay self-employment taxes: the fire
department pays the employer's share of Social Security and
Medicare taxes on her wage earnings. Sally knows that she will
be responsible for these taxes if she works for herself and
therefore counts them as part of her current compensation. Table
2-4 summarizes the results of her calculations.

Table 2-4: Opportunity Cost of Time for a Part-Time Worker

Compensation	Hours per Month	Monthly Earnings	Annual Earnings
Shift			
Weekend - daytime	16 hours	$248.98	$2,988
Weekend - nights	8 hours	$136.94	$1,643
Weekday - nights	8 hours	$117.04	$1,404
Total Wages	32 hours	$502.95	$6,035
Social Security (6.2%)		$31.18	$374
Medicare (1.45%)		$7.29	$88
Total Compensation		$541.43	$6,497

Summing Up: Sally is now in a better position to evaluate the
benefits of other part-time or full-time occupations. If she goes
to work for herself, she knows that she will have to earn roughly
$6,500 to replace the income she now earns from her work with
the fire department.

KEY POINTS TO REMEMBER:

❑   If you are paid on an hourly basis, shift differentials
    can have a substantial impact on your base hourly
    wage. If you work several different types of shifts,
    your wage per hour on the job will be an average of
    the rates for your various shifts.

❑   If your employer pays its share of Social Security and
    Medicare taxes, but offers no other benefits, then
    your total compensation will be 7.65% higher (i.e.,
    6.2% plus 1.45%) than the amount indicated by your
    wage per hour.

♒ ♒ ♒

COMPUTING HOURLY EARNINGS

As you compare your current earnings with other available
options, it is often helpful to compute your current earnings per
hour *actually worked*. The conventional method of reporting
hourly employee earnings can be quite misleading. In this
section, you will learn how to use the annual earnings estimates
developed earlier in this chapter to compute a measure of your
earnings that can be sensibly compared with consulting billing
rates and with earnings from other forms of self-employment.

It is common to report employee earnings per hour as an
annual base salary divided by 2080 – the *total* number of hours
available in a 52-week year.[5]   For example, in 2001 the U.S.
Office of Personal Management (or OPM) – the entity which
oversees the Civil Service pay and benefits structure – quotes the
annual salary for a mid-range GS-14 division chief working in
Seattle as $84,827 and the corresponding hourly rate as $46.40
for 2001.[6] Nevertheless, this compensation measure understates
such a manager's actual earnings per hour worked in two distinct

ways – it fails to adjust for either employee benefits or paid holidays and personal leave. As we will see, the division chief actually earns substantially more per hour worked than the rate quoted by OPM.

Let's start by computing the division chief's expected total compensation for the year 2001. (We can later estimate her future compensation – the opportunity cost of quitting – by allowing for expected inflation.) Let's also assume that this division chief currently receives – and would choose to maintain – the typical package of employee benefits identified by the Office of Management and Budget (OMB).[7] Using the benefit rates specified by OMB, we see in Table 2-5 that the division chief's expected *annual* compensation is higher than her base salary by more than one-third.

Table 2-5: Total Compensation in the Federal Civil Service

	OMB Rate	Amount
Base Salary: GS-14, Step 5 in Seattle, WA		$84,827
Retirement Benefits	23.70%	$20,104
Insurance	5.70%	$4,835
Medicare	1.45%	$1,230
Miscellaneous	1.70%	$1,442
TOTAL		**$112,438**

The OMB scenario also provides us with an expected number of work hours for a typical civil servant. More specifically, OMB Circular A-76 requires you to assume – when comparing public and private sector employees – that an average Federal employee works 1776 hours per year. Let's assume that this average reflects the amount of time spent on the job by our division chief in Seattle. Table 2-6 details the implications of this assumption for hourly earnings – the division chief earns $63.31 per hour actually worked, an amount over 36 percent higher than the official rate quoted by OPM.

Table 2-6: Federal Civil Service Hourly Earnings

Total Annual Compensation, GS-14, Step 5 in Seattle, WA	$112,438
Hours Worked per Year	1776
Earnings per Hour Worked	**$63.31**

This finding provides an important illustration of the adjustments you need to make when comparing your earnings as an employee with your anticipated hourly consulting rates or earnings from business activities. Since consultants and business owners do not get paid holidays or personal leave, you must always quote employee compensation rates in terms that are consistent with other business conventions. In general, your first step is to compute your total expected employee compensation (as we did earlier for Beverly, Fran and Sally). Your relevant hourly rate is then found by dividing your employee compensation by the number of hours you spend on the job each year. The cases we analyzed earlier provide useful illustrations of this approach.

Let's first return to the case of Beverly, the CPA employed by a small accounting firm. Since her employer gives her 10 paid holidays and 12 personal leave days per year, she works a total of 1904 hours per year. As Table 2-7 shows, Beverly currently earns $40.44 per hour on the job. This amount represents what Beverly would have to earn per hour as an independent contractor or small business owner in order to replicate her current compensation – assuming that she continues to work the same number of hours once she is on her own. Of course, if she ends up working *more* hours, her break-even rate would be lower. By similar reasoning, if she worked *fewer* hours, Beverly's break-even rate would rise.

Table 2-7: Expected Earnings per Hour, Salaried Employee

Item	Description	Hours
Total hours available per year	52 weeks; 40 hours per week	2080
less		
Holidays	10 days per year	80
Personal Days	12 days per year	96
Total hours actually worked		1904
Total expected earnings	from Table 2-1	$77,003
Earnings per Hour worked	earnings ÷ hours	$40.44

The calculations for Fran, a full-time employee paid by the hour, are somewhat more complicated. Once again, it is necessary to use the hours actually worked as the basis for your analysis. Given the number of holidays and leave days Fran generally takes and the overtime she usually works, it turns out that she typically spends 1992 hours per year on the job. In this case, her expected earnings per hour actually worked are $29.37, an amount 25 percent higher than her base hourly rate of $23.50. Table 2-8 provides the details of these calculations. In other words, Fran would have to be paid $29.37 per hour as an independent contractor to replicate her current level of compensation – assuming that she continues to work the same number of hours once she is on her own.

Table 2-8: Expected Earnings per Hour, Hourly Employee

Item	Description	Hours
Total hours available per year	52 weeks; 40 hours per week	2080
less		
Holidays	10 days per year	80
Personal Days	13 days per year	104
plus		
Overtime	one 8-hour shift per month	96
Total hours actually worked		**1992**
Total expected annual earnings	from Table 2-2	**$58,511**
Earnings per hour worked	earnings ÷ hours	**$29.37**

The calculations for Sally, a part-time worker, are somewhat more straight-forward. We know from Table 2-4 that Sally works an average of 32 hours a month. It follows that she works 384 hours in a typical year. As Table 2-9 demonstrates, Sally earns an average of $16.92 per hour on the job, an amount 27 percent higher than her base hourly rate. In other words, Sally would have to be paid $16.92 per hour as an independent contractor in order to replicate her current earnings from part-time employment – assuming that the number of hours she works remains unchanged.

Table 2-9: Expected Earnings per Hour Worked, Part-Time
          Worker

Total hours actually worked	384
Total expected annual earnings	$6,497
Earnings per hour worked	$16.92

In the cases we have discussed thus far, each employee's compensation per hour worked was substantially higher than her hourly wage rate as conventionally computed. A comparison of these cases reveals several distinct sources for this discrepancy:

- non-wage benefits
- paid holidays and personal leave days
- overtime pay differentials and
- evening, night, and weekend shift differentials.

It is essential to include *all* forms of current compensation – including those not included in your hourly wage – when you are placing a value on the status quo.

KEY POINT TO REMEMBER:

❑ To compare employee compensation with contractor hourly rates, you must compute the amount an employee earns per hour worked: total employee compensation divided by total hours on the job per year.

❄ ❄ ❄

TRY IT YOURSELF!

You now have enough information to compute out *your* total compensation, both on an hourly and an annual basis. Table 2-10 provides a template for figuring out these amounts for salaried employees. Table 2-11 provides a comparable template for employees who are paid on an hourly basis. These tables will help you determine the opportunity cost of *leaving* your current job. In the next chapter, we examine such opportunity cost questions in greater depth, looking at both the financial consequences of *modifying* your current job as well as the financial implications of choosing an entirely new occupation.

Table 2-10: Total Compensation for *Salaried* Employees

Type of Compensation	Rate (if any)	Annual Amount
Base Salary		
Overtime/Pay for Extra Projects		
Bonus/Merit Raise		
Cost of Living Increase		
FICA[8] (employer's share of tax on first $80,400)	.062	
Medicare (employer's share)	.0145	
Retirement (employer's contribution)		
Health Insurance (employer's contribution and price difference if any)		
Life Insurance (employer's contribution and price difference if any)		
Disability Insurance(employer's contribution and price difference if any)		
Employer's subsidy for employee business expenses		
Other Benefits (your replacement cost)		
TOTAL ANNUAL COMPENSATON		
Total hours available per year		2080
less		
Holidays		
Personal Days		
Other Paid Days Off		
Compensatory Leave Days taken		
plus		
Overtime hours (paid or unpaid)		
Compensatory Leave Days earned		
TOTAL HOURS ON THE JOB		
EARNINGS PER HOUR ON THE JOB *(total compensation divided by total hours)*		

Table 2-11: Total Compensation for Employees Paid by the Hour

Compensation Type (annual basis)	Hours	Rate	Amount
Wages Earned			
Hours on the job at base rate			
Hours on the job at weekend rate			
Hours on the job at evening rate			
Hours on the job at night rate			
Paid holiday hours			
Paid personal leave hours			
Other Paid leave hours			
Overtime hours worked			
Bonus/Merit Award (one-time payment)			
Non-Wage Benefits	Rate		
FICA[9] (employer's share of tax on first \$80,400)			
Medicare (employer's share)			
Retirement (employer's contribution)			
Health Insurance (employer's contribution and price difference if any)			
Life Insurance (employer's contribution and price difference if any)			
Disability Insurance (employer's contribution and price difference if any)			
Employer's subsidy for employee expenses			
Other Benefits			
TOTAL ANNUAL COMPENSATION			

Table 2-11 (continued)

Hours Worked:	
Hours at base pay	
Evening, night, and weekend hours	
Overtime hours	
TOTAL HOURS ON THE JOB	
EARNINGS PER HOUR ON THE JOB (total compensation divided by total hours)	

≈ ≈ ≈

─────────── ENDNOTES ───────────

[1] Unless otherwise indicated, the case examples used in this book are *hypothetical* – based on realistic prices and costs but not representing the personal circumstances of any one individual. The salary and wage rates cited in this chapter are based on regional data reported by salary.com for Spring 2001.

[2] When you undertake a similar exercise, you may not know precisely how much extra your health insurance will cost. In these circumstances, the best you can do is to figure out how much extra you *expect* to pay – based on the COBRA option available through your employer or a group rate through a professional association, school alumni association, or perhaps a similar organization offering benefits to members.

[3] Under the terms of Sally's employment contract, shift differentials for nights, evenings, and weekends are applied to each other. For example, when Sally works a night shift on a weekend, the 17 percent weekend premium is applied to both

Sally's base pay and to the 10 percent night differential. The hourly rate with both differentials is computed as $13.30 x 1.17 x 1.10, an amount that is 28.7 percent higher than her base wage.

[4] Since the shift differentials specified in Sally's contract are defined as percentages of her base wage, the extra income she earns by working nights and weekends grows as her base wage increases. Some employers have sought to limit the size of shift differentials by specifying dollar amounts (instead of percentage increases) for working less desirable shifts. In such a system, working at night would increase your hourly wage by a fixed amount – for example, $2 – instead of a fixed percentage such as 10 percent.

[5] Of course, a 365-day year actually gives us 52 weeks plus one day, or 2087 hours per year. Nevertheless, many employers use 2080 hours for convenience.

[6] This hourly rate is computed using a 2087-hour work-year.

[7] This benefits package is described in OMB Circular A-76, *Performance of Commercial Activities,* the document that lays out the methodology to be used when comparing Federal civil service employees with individuals working in the private sector.

[8] Although Congress rarely changes the FICA tax *rate* of 6.2 percent, the amount of income subject to this tax increases annually as it is adjusted for inflation. The amount of income subject to this tax was $80,400 for the 2001 tax year.

[9] Although Congress rarely changes the FICA tax *rate* of 6.2 percent, the amount of income subject to this tax increases annually as it is adjusted for inflation. The amount of income subject to this tax was $80,400 for the 2001 tax year.

Hour by Hour: Working as a Contractor

Once you have figured out how much you currently earn, the next question naturally becomes, "How much do I need to charge if I bill clients by the hour?" We cover two approaches to this question here. The first uses only previous earnings as a benchmark for choosing a billing rate, while the second relies on opportunity cost analysis to adjust fees for differences among jobs in the *quality* of the work environment.

A comparison of these approaches provides an important lesson: hourly compensation is *not* a complete measure of available job alternatives. For example,

- a position with an hourly billing rate above your current earnings per hour may not provide you with enough work to generate the income you would like to have; and

- a position with an hourly billing rate below your current earnings per hour may offer personal advantages that offset its financial consequences.

This chapter will show you how to take these considerations into account when evaluating your options. This technique is applicable to a wide variety of situations: you can use exactly the same logic to plan a new career as an interior decorator or a tax advisor, a management consultant or an agency nurse. In each case, you will have to decide how much you need to charge for your time.

☙ ☙ ☙

JUST BREAKING EVEN

Scenario Background: Our Chapter 2 discussion of Fran's position as a hospital employee[1] provides a context for our analysis of break-even billing rates. As an R.N., Fran has the option of exchanging her employee status for that of an "agency nurse." If she chooses to restructure her job in this way, she would essentially become an independent contractor selling professional services. When analyzing Fran's choices, it is important to remember that the approach we use applies to virtually all independent contractors. Only the personal details change, not the underlying logic of the method.

As we noted earlier, Fran earns $23.50 as a base hourly wage for her work as a full-time R.N. However, as an *employee*, she is currently paid for more than just the hours spent on the job: she also earns paid holidays, personal leave days and a variety of non-wage benefits. After taking these benefits into account, we found that Fran can expect to earn $58,511 if she stays at her current job next year, and we interpreted this amount as her opportunity cost of quitting. In other words, if Fran were able to earn $58,511 as an independent contractor, then she would be able to replace her current take-home pay and maintain her current level of employee benefits.

Since Fran now works 1,992 hours per year to earn $58,511, it follows that her expected compensation per hour *on the job* would be $29.37 if she stayed at her current job for the coming year. However, this amount is not necessarily what she would need to charge as a contractor if she wishes to replace her current income.

Letters of Agreement: Many independent contractors sign "letters of agreement" that specify an hourly rate or fee, but do not guarantee a minimum number of hours per year. Our opportunity cost analysis is readily modified to help you evaluate this contract form.

We already know that Fran's expected compensation is $58,511 for next year. The number of hours she needs to work as a contractor in order to replace this sum will, of course, depend on her hourly fee. Fran knows that two of her friends work as agency nurses; one earns $28 per hour while the other receives $31 per hour. Fran knows that she could obtain a position similar to these if she chose. Table 3-1 summarizes her initial analysis of these two opportunities.

Table 3-1: Contractor Hours to Replace Current Compensation

Target Compensation: $58,511	Rate Offered	Break-Even Hours
Case 1: Current Earnings/Hr.	$29.37	1,992
Case 2: Hourly rate below current earnings/hr.	$28.00	2,090
Case 3: Hourly rate above current earnings/hr.	$31.00	1,887

In general, she computes her break-even number of hours by dividing the hourly fee offered into her target compensation of $58,511. Not surprisingly, she finds that the higher the hourly fee, the lower the break-even number of hours.

Fran's final assessment of these contracts will depend on the hourly fee offered, the number of hours she expects to work, and the value she currently places on personal time.

- Case 1 represents the status quo and thus provides our point of comparison.

- Even though the contract in Case 2 offers an hourly rate above Fran's current base wage of $23.50, the contract rate is below what she currently earns per hour on the job. In other words, if she wanted to replace her current income, she would have to work longer hours. Unless this job provides significant non-monetary advantages over the status quo, Fran is likely to be *worse off* with this contract than she is in her current position.

- The contract in Case 3 does enable Fran to replace her current income as long as she is able to work at least 1,887 hours per year.   Unless this position has significant non-monetary *dis*advantages, Fran is likely to end up *better off* with this contract than she is now.

Although we can make an educated guess at how Fran would rank these three options, her ultimate ranking of these contracts will be ambiguous – as long as we fail to take job quality into account. By "job quality" we mean personal circumstances such as

- the personal value or cost of any additional hours on the job. For example, a contract requiring more time on the job may force Fran to spend more on child care or may simply prevent her from spending sanity-preserving time with her family and friends.

- the personal value or benefit of any additional discretionary/free time. For example, a change in hours spent on the job or commuting to and from the office may save Fran money on child care or may simply give her the luxury of spending more time with the important people in her life.

- the personal value of any changes in job-related expenditures such as lower dry-cleaning bills and office lunch expenses, or higher home office supply costs.

The specific values that Fran assigns to these job quality issues will necessarily reflect her personal tastes, values and financial situation. In each case, she has to come up with a *subjective* personal value that indicates how much salary she is willing to give up to obtain a non-monetary benefit (or how much money she needs in order to accept a non-monetary hassle).

Naturally, the specific amount will depend on her tastes and her individual circumstances. Someone with greater personal resources will often be willing to give up more money in order to have more free time or a more flexible work schedule. In other words, a wealthier individual will often place a higher subjective value on non-monetary benefits. Other personal circumstances may also influence this subjective value. A person with care-giving responsibilities for young children or an aging parent at home may place a higher value on the ability to telecommute. Someone just starting a career may place a higher value on opportunities for promotion. The common thread is that these subjective values depend on the details of the status quo.

In the next section, we look at one way Fran could combine financial and quality of life information – once she has decided on the importance she places of the non-monetary aspects of the job.

KEY POINT TO REMEMBER:

❑   Compute the minimum number of hours needed to replace your current income as a ratio:

$$\left(\begin{array}{c} \textbf{Min. Hrs.} \\ \textbf{Needed} \end{array} \right) = \left(\begin{array}{c} \textbf{Current Total} \\ \textbf{Compensation} \end{array} \right) \div \left(\begin{array}{c} \textbf{Hourly Rate} \\ \textbf{Offered} \end{array} \right)$$

In other words, divide your total current compensation by the hourly rate offered in the contract you are considering.

☷ ☷ ☷

FINDING EQUAL JOB SATISFACTION

Let us suppose that Fran has three more options to consider. Each offer defines a distinct case with its own implied work schedule, hourly rate and personal consequences.

- If she accepts the contract defined in Case 4, Fran would sign a letter of agreement specifying an hourly rate of $27, an amount *below* her current earnings per hour. In this case, she expects to work roughly the same schedule she now has – 1990 hours per year. In addition, this position offers her substantially more opportunity for independence and self direction, conditions that Fran treats as a *benefit* worth $5000 per year. In other words, given her current situation Fran is willing to give up $5000 in order to gain more independence on the job.

- In Case 5, Fran would sign a letter of agreement with an hourly rate of $30.50, an amount *above* her current earnings per hour. In this case, she expects to work *more* hours than she now does. The greater pressure of this work environment constitutes an annual personal *cost* of $3500 for Fran. In other words, given her current situation Fran requires an additional $3500 before she would be willing to change the status quo and accept the greater pressure on the job.

- If she accepts the contract defined in Case 6, Fran would sign a letter of agreement promising her an hourly rate of $35, an amount substantially above her current earnings per hour. In this case she also expects to work far fewer billable hours per year – an average of only 30 hours a week for 52 weeks a year. She thinks of the extra free time in this scenario as a non-wage *benefit* worth $2000. In other words, given her current circumstances Fran would be willing to accept a $2000 pay cut in order to have extra free time.

Fran knows that she can choose no more than one of these options. To compare them, she needs to figure out how to combine three types of information: the expected schedule, the hourly promised hourly rate and a dollar value that reflects the personal implications of the new job experience.

As she analyzes each case, Fran attempts to find combinations of work hours and billing rates that would allow her to realize at least the same level of job satisfaction that she now enjoys. She does this in two stages. She first adjusts her target monetary compensation to allow for non-wage benefits. In other words, she subtracts non-wage *benefits* and adds non-wage *costs* to her target monetary compensation – this enables her to determine how much she must money earn per year to achieve her current level of job satisfaction.

Table 3-2: Computing a Minimum Desired Hourly Rate

	Case 4	Case 5	Case 6
Target Compensation (Status Quo)	$58,511	$58,511	$58,511
less **Non-wage *benefit* of new position**	$5,000		$2,000
plus **Non-wage *cost* of new position**		$3,500	
Adjusted target compensation	$53,511	$62,011	$56,511
Expected hours on the job	1,990	2000	1560
Minimum desired hourly rate for this job	$26.89	$31.01	$36.23
Contract Rate Offered	$27.00	$30.50	$35.00
Preferable to Status Quo?	YES	NO	NO

Once Fran has found the relevant target income for a given case, she uses the expected scheduling information to compute her minimum desired hourly rate. Table 3-2 provides the details of her calculations.

Same Schedule, Lower Reservation Billing Rate: As we mentioned earlier, Fran currently works 1,992 hours per year and expects to earn an average of $29.37 per hour on the job next year.[2] The contract defined in Case 4 offers essentially the same schedule and a significant non-wage *benefit* relative to the status quo. As a result, Fran feels that she would be better off with the new job even if the hourly contract rate were somewhat lower than her current earnings per hour.   In particular, she would be happier with the new job as long as she expect to earn at least $53,511 per year.   If she works 1990 hours per year, this translates into an hourly rate at or above of $26.89.   This minimum desired rate is also known as her *reservation billing rate* – Fran's lowest acceptable hourly rate. Since the contract actually offers her $27, this option represents an improvement over the status quo.

Longer Hours, Higher Reservation Billing Rate: Since Fran expects to work longer and more stressful hours in Case 5, she needs the promise of a higher hourly rate before she would willingly accept this contract. Specifically, her adjusted target compensation is $62,011 and her reservation billing rate is $31.01 for this scenario. Since the Case 5 contract only offers $30.50 per hour, she decides that she would rather have the status quo than this contract.

Fewer Hours, Higher Reservation Billing Rate: It is often the case that life as a full-time independent contractor leaves you with far fewer than 40 *billable* hours per week. Under the contract in Case 6, Fran expects to have 30 billable hours per week, for a total of 1560 hours per year. She places a value of $2000 per year on the extra free time she enjoys in this scenario. As a result, Fran's adjusted target compensation is $56,511 and her reservation billing rate is $36.23. Since the Case 6 contract offers only $35 per hour, Fran decides that she would again prefer the status quo to this situation.

We can now see how Fran has used the information she had available to make her decision on the basis of opportunity cost. By comparing each offer to the status quo, she was able to compute a minimum acceptable hourly rate for each. Given the terms of the three available offers, Fran discovered that only one (Case 4) was preferable to the status quo. Thus, her analysis leads her to choose the contract described in Case 4. If more than one option had been preferable to the status quo she would need to compare these options to each other to reach a final decision. At the end of this chapter you will find the forms and instructions needed to tackle such decisions on your own.

KEY POINTS TO REMEMBER:

❑   If a position offers a non-wage *benefit*, you should *subtract* this benefit from your initial target compensation to find your adjusted target compensation.

❑   If a contract implies non-wage *costs*, you should *add* this cost to your initial target compensation to find your adjusted target compensation.

❑   Divide your adjusted target compensation by the expected number of hours to find your reservation wage.

≋   ≋   ≋

WORKING AS A PART-TIME CONTRACTOR:

The question of whether or not to take on part-time work is yet another situation in which opportunity cost analysis can help you make the most effective use of your time. As before, this approach has you compare the value of your current activities with the value to you of the available alternatives. In other words, you need to figure out exactly what would change in your life if you took a part-time job and compare this with the benefits you hope to gain from the new source of income. Once again, we can use Fran's overtime schedule to illustrate this technique.

Target Compensation for Part-Time Work: In this example, let's assume that Fran is considering cutting back on overtime hours and getting a part-time job elsewhere. The primary difference between this case and the ones discussed in the previous section lies in the method of computing the initial target compensation. Fran's compensation per hour of overtime differs considerably from her average overall compensation per hour on the job. There are two basic reasons for this: -

- Fran's base hourly rate is higher for overtime hours than for her regular shifts.

- Some benefits – including life insurance, disability insurance, and reimbursement for professional expenses – are not linked to her overtime hours. Since these benefits remain the same even if Fran cuts her out overtime hours altogether, they do not count as part of the opportunity cost of her overtime compensation.

To compute Fran's earnings per hour of overtime, we start by calculating how much she earns directly from these extra shifts. Table 3-3 provides the results of these computations.

We know that Fran is paid $37.60 per overtime hour and that she works an average of 8 hours per month, for a total of 96 hours and $3,610 per year. In addition, Fran's employer pays its share of Social Security and Medicare taxes. As before, we treat these taxes as a benefit since Fran would have to pay them herself if she were to become an independent contractor. Under the terms of Fran's current employment, none of her other benefits are linked to overtime hours. We can therefore ignore them as we compute her overtime earnings.

Table 3-3 Part-Time Earnings for an Hourly Employee

Type of Compensation	Nature of Payment	Value
Fran's Overtime Hours	$37.6 per hour of weekend overtime; 8 hours worked per month	$3,610
FICA (employer's share)	6.2% of cash compensation	$223.80
Medicare (employer's share)	1.45% of cash compensation	$52.34
	TOTAL	$3,886
	HOURLY RATE	$40

Adding her wages to the value of the relevant benefits, we see that Fran expects to earn a total of $3,886 by working overtime. In other words, Fran would stand to loose $3,886 next year if she stopped working extra shifts. This amount represents the opportunity cost to her of changing the status quo by accepting a part-time job as a contractor elsewhere.

Fran can now compare this opportunity cost with her available alternatives using the reservation billing rate discussed in the previous section. As before, her ultimate choice will depend on both the financial and personal impact of the change. Part-time contract jobs that offer greater independence or the chance to learn about new opportunities may be preferable to the status quo even if they pay somewhat less per hour.

KEY POINT TO REMEMBER:

❑   Compare your earnings from a new part-time job with the *change* (if any) in your current earnings as an employee.

❀ ❀ ❀

TRY IT YOURSELF!

You now have the background you need to compute your own reservation hourly rate for either full-time or part-time work as an independent contractor. For each contract, you would start by computing your initial target annual compensation – the amount of money your would need to replace the salary and benefits you give up by changing jobs.

Table 3-4: Your Reservation Hourly Billing Rate

	Case
Target Compensation (Status Quo)	
less **Non-wage *benefit* of new position**	
plus **Non-wage *cost* of new position**	
Adjusted target compensation	
Expected hours on the job	
Minimum desired hourly rate for this job	
Contract rate offered	
Is this offer preferable to the status quo?	YES/NO

You would then adjust this for perceived differences between your current situation and the one you expect to find after taking a new position. In other words, you need to figure out how much money you would be willing to give up in order to improve your current working conditions (or how much of a pay raise you would require to accept conditions that are more disagreeable than the status quo). This amount will clearly be subjective -- it will depend on your personal tastes and your current circumstances.

Finally you compute your reservation hourly rate, dividing your adjusted target compensation by the number of billable hours you expect to work in the new job.

♒ ♒ ♒

———————— ENDNOTES ————————

[1] See Table 2-2 and Table 2-8, along with the accompanying text.

[2] See Table 2-2, Table 2-8 and the accompanying text for an explanation of Fran's current compensation.

4

SELLING YOUR PRODUCTS, NOT YOUR TIME

Virtually all businesses start out small – one or two people with a great product or idea that they want to sell. In this chapter, we look at two of the questions confronting all such would-be entrepreneurs:

- Should I go into business for myself?

- Is this particular project a good idea?

To answer these questions, we go back to the notion of *opportunity cost* discussed in Chapter 2 and use it as a guideline for business decisions. We continue to assume that a project makes sense if the benefits you expect to receive exceed the value *to you* of the best of the available alternatives.

Most of the examples we will analyze illustrate the operating decisions typically made by sole proprietors involved in one of three lines of business: professional services, small scale producer, and retail operations. This choice of activities makes it possible to examine a variety of business ventures in both their start-up phases and as fully-established enterprises. Our emphasis on sole proprietors enables us to focus on the *logic* of basic business decisions – and to avoid the complications that result from having to treat the business owner, her board of directors and the company itself as legally distinct entities.

In this chapter we will see how to compare your earnings from the manufacture and sale of products with the other income-producing options available to you. The particular business ventures discussed in this chapter are presented as open-ended contracts -- agreements that allow to produce as much or as little as you choose.

At the heart of each case lies a question requiring a simple yes or no answer: "Is the proposed venture a good idea?" Details such as the nature of the goods you will provide, the price you will be paid and the production methods you will use have already been settled. For now, it is only a question of deciding whether or not to go ahead and accept a particular proposal. In later chapters we expand our decision-making framework to include the task of defining and seeking out new business opportunities – rather than simply reacting to those that come looking for us.

In the next section you will find a general definition of business earnings. In later sections you will have the chance to analyze two business cases. In the first of these scenarios, we calculate potential earnings from making patchwork quilts to illustrate the nature of income earned from a production process. In the second scenario, we expand our notion of opportunity cost to include the value of money as well as labor. We analyze the earnings potential an antiques dealer to illustrate this broader notion of opportunity cost and to provide a general definition of income earned from retail operations. At the end of the chapter you will find templates designed to help you analyze your own business opportunities.

❦ ❦ ❦

BUSINESS EARNINGS AND OPPORTUNITY COSTS IN GENERAL

The basic question of interest in this chapter is similar to the one posed earlier in this book: "Will I earn enough from a proposed business venture to cover my opportunity costs?" The answer to this question requires two types of information: an estimate of your business earnings and an understanding of your current opportunity costs.

The Opportunity Cost of Your Time

Although the context differs slightly from the cases discussed earlier, the method used to compute your opportunity cost remains the same. For any proposed venture you still need to ask the following:

- What are you now doing with the time you would have to devote to the new project? For example, are you

    o working at your regular pay rate?
    o working overtime at your regular job?
    o spending time with family and friends?
    o pursuing leisure activities, volunteer work, etc.?

- What is the value to you of these activities? Specifically,

    o what is your current salary or annual wage (if any)?
    o what is the value to you of your employee benefits (if any)?
    o how would you *feel* about changing the status quo?
    o what are the non-wage benefits and costs of the new situation?

Table 2-10 and Table 2-11 (found on pages 24 and 25) should help you organize the information you need to tackle these questions. Once you have sorted out these details, you will have a sense of how much you would need to earn per hour in a new venture for it to be worthwhile on a part-time or full-time basis. In other words, you will know the *opportunity cost* of the time you will need for this project.

KEY POINT TO REMEMBER:

❑   The *opportunity cost* of the time spent on a project is the value *to you* of the next best use of this resource.

Business Earnings Defined:

The basic questions about the new business opportunity also remain the same as in earlier chapters. They include

- How much money do you expect to earn from the proposed venture?

- What other benefits, if any, do you expect to receive from this activity? Such benefits may include

    o   greater independence, more control over your work,
    o   more flexible scheduling, or
    o   opportunity to work on more interesting projects.

Although the basic questions remain unchanged, you will need to follow a somewhat different approach when calculating your actual business earnings. In particular, your income will no longer be based on an hourly billing rate. Instead, your earnings amount to whatever is left over after you have paid all the bills *directly associated* with the new venture. We will also see that the notion of income needed to make sound business decisions may differ from the definition of income used by the IRS.

KEY POINT TO REMEMBER:

❑ Your gain from a new business venture – your *earnings* from the activity – is defined as the difference between the revenue and the costs *directly* associated with this particular activity.

❧ ❧ ❧

BUSINESS EARNINGS AND OPPORTUNITY COSTS IN PRACTICE

A basic production process – making patchwork quilts for sale to a craft show vendor – helps illustrate how this approach works in practice.

Table 4-1: Earnings from a New Business Venture

Expected Revenue from the Project
less
Cost of Production Materials
Cost of Extra Production Help
Cost of Additional Equipment
Cost of Additional Professional Services
Additional Marketing and Administrative Costs
equals
Your Earnings from this Activity

The general definition of your earnings is fairly straightforward: it amounts to whatever money remains after you have paid all expenses directly associated with making quilts. Table 4-1 provides a more detailed version of this definition and lists some general categories of expenses. Although this notion of your earnings is simple in structure, it may be somewhat complicated to use. The difficulty lies in identifying the precise expenses that you need to consider as you decide whether or not to start making quilts for sale.

Identifying Relevant Costs: In general, you want to decide whether or not the financial and personal benefits to be gained from this venture are more valuable to *you* than whatever you would have to give up to pursue this opportunity. Basic business principles (and common sense) indicate that you should look only at those costs (and benefits) that *change* when you choose a new course of action. Economic and financial analysts often call this method an "*incremental cost*" or "*marginal cost*" approach to project evaluation. With this general approach, you will be able to find out which projects bring in enough revenue to cover their costs – and add to your bottom line. By encouraging you to examine the direct consequences of specific changes, it helps you select the best of the available alternatives.

The easiest way to figure out whether or not to include a particular expense in your analysis is to ask yourself the two questions listed in Table 4-2.

Table 4-2: Expenses Associated with New Business Ventures

Will I incur this expense if I go ahead with the venture?	*YES*	NO
Will I incur this expense if I *do not* go ahead with the venture?	YES	*NO*

If you answered "Yes" to the first question and "No" to the second question, then the expense *is* directly associated with the project and should be included. It *is* one that you incur only if you go ahead with the new venture. Examples of such expenses for a quilt maker would include the cost of fabric, thread, and any other supplies needed to produce the final product, as well as the cost of any additional employees, contractors, or services needed to help with the manufacturing process.[1]

KEY POINT TO REMEMBER:

❑ The expenses directly relevant to your business decision are those costs which you incur if and only if you undertake the project in question.

Costs to Ignore: If you are stuck with a particular cost no matter what you decide about a given business proposal, you might as well ignore the cost when making your business decision. Such expenditures are often called "sunk" or "fixed" costs to indicate that they cannot be readily avoided. Since these costs remain the same in any case, they are not relevant to the question at hand. (Worrying about them might give you gray hair, but it won't help you increase your earnings!)

In our quilt-making example, such costs would include the expenses associated with existing business ventures or expenses that do not change with the mix of new and old activities, such as rent on existing facilities, payments on existing equipment leases and current administrative support costs. All these expenditures represent costs that you would bear no matter what you decide about the quilt-making proposal. Since these costs are unaffected by the status of the quilt-making project, they should have no bearing on your decision.

KEY POINT TO REMEMBER:

❑   If a cost does not change as the result of a business
     decision, it should be ignored when making that
     decision.

Scenario 1: Making Quilts for a Craft Fair Vendor

We now turn to the details of the quilt-making process. A craft
show vendor has indicated that she is willing to buy up to ten
quilts from you at a price of $350 each. She promises to provide
you with the pattern and the full-sized templates you need to
make quilts for a queen-size bed. As an experienced quilter, you
know that it takes you 10 hours to make such a quilt by machine.
You also realize that this new business venture will require some
additional record-keeping and administrative chores – an average
of 1 hour per quilt.

     You already have all the other necessary space and
equipment – an appropriate sewing machine, scissors, rotary
cutters, rulers, etc. The only additional expense that you would
incur to produce these quilts is the cost of fabric, thread, and
batting (filling). A queen-size quilt requires 14 yards of cotton
fabric. The cloth you want to use is on sale for 25 percent off its
usual price of $8.98 per yard.

 - Since the sale implies that the fabric is available at
   75 percent (.75) of its usual price, your fabric cost
   per quilt is 14 x (.75) x $8.98 = $94.29

The other materials you need cost $12 per quilt.

     You are now ready to sit down and compute your earnings
per hour from this quilt-making project. In this example, you
know how much revenue you would receive for a single quilt,

the amount of time required, and the additional costs incurred. As Table 4-3 demonstrates, your net income of $243.71 per quilt provides you with an hourly rate of $243.71/11=$22.16.

Table 4-3: Hourly Earnings per Quilt

Item	Description	Amount
Quilt price received	payment from retailer	$350
less		
Quilt fabric cost	14 yards at $8.98 per yard, on sale at 25% off regular price	$94.29
Other materials cost	thread and batting/fill	$12
Net earnings per quilt		$243.71
Hourly rate	11 hours to complete project	$22.16

Reaching a Decision: Should you go ahead and make quilts for the craft show vendor? As before, the answer depends on the value *to you* of your time. In other words, it depends on whether the benefits you expect from the quilt-making project are at least as great as the opportunity cost of the time you would need to complete the work.

The general decision-making process recommended here is the same as the one used to evaluate the available options in Chapter 3. Once you know what extra revenue and expenses to expect, you can figure out the financial consequences of changing the status quo. When you combine this with your view of the personal consequences of the venture, you can make your final choice on the basis of opportunity cost. Following the approach recommended throughout this book, *you should accept the proposal if the benefit you expect to receive is greater than the opportunity cost of the time and materials required for the project.*

It is important to remember that this decision process works even if you do not have as much information as the above example pre-supposed. You may not know exactly how long the quilt will take to piece together, how much the fabric will cost, how much time you will have to spend on administrative chores, or how long it will take to get paid. In such cases, the best you can do is rely on the most accurate information reasonably available – and use it to figure out what you *expect* the project to require in both time and money.

The Nature of your Decision: Our opportunity cost method does not require an "all-or-nothing" answer. Given the terms of the vendor's offer – a fixed price per quilt for up to 10 quilts – you may decide to produce fewer than the maximum number that the vendor is willing to buy. Table 4-4 shows how earnings vary with the number of quilts sold. As you can see, *total* earnings for this project grow with the number of hours spent quilting, while earnings *per hour* remain constant.

Table 4-4: Potential Earnings from Quilt Production

Quilts Made	Earnings per Quilt	Total Earnings	Hours Required	Earnings per Hour
2	$243.71	$487.42	22	$22.16
4	$243.71	$974.84	44	$22.16
6	$243.71	$1,462.26	66	$22.16
8	$243.71	$1,949.68	88	$22.16
10	$243.71	$2,437.10	110	$22.16

However, it is not likely that the opportunity cost of your time will be constant. In other words, you may have at least a few hours with a relatively low opportunity cost – ones that could be devoted to a new venture with only minor adjustments in your current activities. Let's assume for the moment that your earnings per hour of $22.16 represents the *full* benefit you anticipate from quilting. If you have 25 hours with an opportunity cost below $22.16, then you could decide to make 2 quilts rather than 10. In general, if you want to realize the greatest possible benefit from your time, you should devote to quilting any hour with an opportunity cost below $22.16 (up to a maximum of 110 hours in this example).

Further Examples: Let's consider how such opportunity cost calculations work in more detail. Table 4-5 summarizes the current expected earnings of the three women we discussed in Chapter 2. As we see, two of the women expect to earn more per hour in their current jobs than they would earn from the quilting venture. However, this does not mean that they would necessarily turn down the chance to make at least a few quilts for the vendor.

Table 4-5: Opportunity Cost Summary

	Annual Compensation	Hourly Compensation
Beverly, Full-time CPA	$77,003	$40.44
Fran, Full-time RN	$58,511	$29.37
Sally, Part-time EMT	$6,497	$16.92

The benefits of the quilting venture may still exceed the opportunity cost of time for either Beverly or Fran or both. One or both of them could have personal time that she would be willing to devote to a new occupation – one that provides a complete break from current routines. In such a situation, the opportunity cost of time devoted to quilting would be far lower than *average* compensation from a current job: the quilter would not actually be giving up any current income. One or both of these women may also be curious about the growing market for hand-made goods and thinking about starting her own businesses. The quilting project would then become a way to get a taste of life in this new field. In this case, the benefit per hour to be derived from quilting could be quite large – even though the amount of money earned per hour is small when compared with current wages.

KEY POINTS TO REMEMBER:

❑   Accept new proposals as long as the benefits anticipated exceed your opportunity cost of the time required.

❑   Base your analysis on the costs and benefits *directly* attributable to the project under consideration.

Scenario 2: Running an Antiques Business:

For a second example, we turn to a retailing opportunity – the chance to sell imported antique tiles from a showcase in an "antique mall". The basic logic used to evaluate this venture is essentially the same as the approach used in Scenario 1 to analyze a manufacturing opportunity. Your earnings are again defined to be the amount left over after all direct expenses have been covered. However, the need to maintain an inventory of goods on hand raises a new cash-flow consideration: you must now allow for the passage of time between paying bills and receiving sales revenue. This new wrinkle provides a useful opportunity: it enables us to broaden our discussion to include the opportunity cost of *money* in the context of a relatively simple example.

There are four major expense categories – other than the value of your time – for this business venture: the cost of the tiles themselves, the cost of shipping the tiles to the United States, the rent and sales commissions paid for your showcase in an antique mall, and the opportunity cost of the money you have invested in your business. We examine each of these expenditures in turn.

Cost of Goods Sold: You know that an English dealer will sell you a variety of antique tiles at a price of $70 per tile. You also know that it will cost $11 per tile to ship your order to the United States.

- Your "cost of goods sold" is $70 + $11 = $81 per tile.

For the purposes of this example, let's assume that you order tiles from this dealer once a year and that you pay when the order is placed. You also expect to sell all tiles ordered within one year of purchase

Rent and Sales Commission: Since you expect to maintain a relatively modest inventory, you do not need much space to display your wares. Antique malls can provide a cost-effective means of starting a small-scale antiques business: dealers typically rent booth or showcase space on a monthly basis from a mall operator and pay the operator a small commission on all sales. In exchange, the mall operator maintains the retail space, hires sales staff and handles customer sales on behalf of dealers. You know that you can rent the necessary showcase space for $27 a month at a popular antique mall near your home, and that you will have to pay a 4 percent (or .04) commission on all sales handled by the mall staff. Again for the purposes of this example, let's assume that you rent your showcase for a full year and pay in advance.

- Your annual rental expense is 12 x $27 = $324.

You expect the mall operator to pay you at the end of the year – after she has deducted the her commission from the money collected from your customers.

- If you expect to sell tiles at a price of $125 each, a 4 percent sales commission amounts to .04 x $125 = $5 per tile.

- If you expect to sell tiles at a price of $125 each, your net revenue (or revenue less sales commission) will be $125 - $5 = $120 per tile.

Opportunity Cost of Your Investment: In this scenario, our cost assumptions imply that all expenses are paid immediately, while all revenues are received one year later. This difference in timing will require you to commit financial resources – either personal or borrowed – to your new business. Since money, like time, is typically scarce, you will need to take the opportunity cost of such funds into account when deciding whether or not to go ahead with the project.

To estimate this cost for our antiques business, we must start by calculating the actual amount of money invested – in other words, the actual amount spent on inventory and showcase rental fees. The specific amount invested will, of course, depend on the size of inventory we plan to purchase. Let us suppose that you expect to sell roughly one tile a month and therefore decide to order 12 tiles at the beginning of the year.

- Your initial investment in your new antiques business would be $1,296, the sum of your annual rent payment ($324), the purchase price of your inventory ($70 x 12 = $840) and the cost of shipping your inventory to the U.S. ($11 x 12 = $132).

For the personal financial assets you invest in a new business, the appropriate opportunity cost measure is the amount that the funds could have earned if they had been invested elsewhere. If you took this money out of your personal savings, then its opportunity cost would be the amount of interest, dividends, or capital gains you forego when transferring the money to another use. If you borrow some or all of the money needed, then the opportunity cost will include the interest paid to your lender.

Let us suppose that you decide to cash in some government bonds you now own in order to raise the money needed. If these bonds are now paying 5 percent per year, then the opportunity cost of your initial investment will be 5 percent of $1,296.

- The opportunity cost of investing $1,296 in a new business is .05 x $1296 = $20.25 assuming that the next best alternative investment offers a return of 5 percent per year.

If you financed a larger initial inventory in this fashion, your opportunity cost would be calculated as 5 percent of a larger initial expenditure. If your current return on your savings is other than 5 percent, then your opportunity cost would be calculated using the actual percentage.

Time Commitments: At this point, the only missing ingredient is an estimate of the time that you would need to spend on this new venture. One of the virtues of renting a showcase is that there is always someone else on hand to handle your customer transactions. Nevertheless, you still expect to have administrative chores connected with the business that will average two hours a month. In other words, you expect to spend roughly 2 x 12 = 24 hours per year on the business.

Covering All of Your Opportunity Costs: You are now ready to sit down and figure out how much you could earn from this initial foray into the antiques business. You know that tiles similar to the ones you wish to sell are available elsewhere for $125 each. Table 4-6 indicates how much you would earn – both per hour and in total – if you matched this price.

Table 4-6: Earnings from Selling Antiques

Number of Tiles Sold per Year:	1	6	12	24	36
Revenue	125	750	1500	3000	4500
less:					
Wholesale cost	70	420	840	1680	2520
Shipping cost	11	66	132	264	396
Showcase rental	324	324	324	324	324
Sales Commission	5	30	60	120	180
Opportunity cost of investment (5% of funds committed)	20.25	40.50	64.80	113.40	162.00
Total earnings per year	-305.25	-130.50	79.20	498.60	918.00
Earnings per hour	-$12.72	-$5.44	$3.30	$20.78	$38.25

As the table indicates, you will be able to cover your non-labor costs for the year if you sell an average of one tile per month: at this point, your revenue exceeds these expenses by roughly $80 per year. In other words, you will earn about $3.30 per hour spent on this project if you sell one tile per month (or 12 per year). You will be able to earn slightly more than $20 per hour if you sell two tiles per month (or 24 per year).

Does it make sense to go ahead with the project? Again, the answer depends on the actual number of sales you expect, your own opportunity cost of the time needed, along with any non-monetary benefits you expect from you involvement in this new venture. As before, the project makes sense for people who will derive more satisfaction from this activity than from the available alternatives.

In the next chapter, we address the question of choosing the *best* option from among the available alternatives.

KEY POINTS TO REMEMBER:

❑   Include the opportunity cost of your money, as well
    as your time, in your analysis of new business
    ventures.

❑   The opportunity cost investing your own money in a
    business is equal to what these funds would have
    earned (in interest, dividends and/or capital gains) if
    they had been invested elsewhere.

❊ ❊ ❊

TAXABLE INCOME AND GAINS FROM NEW VENTURES

It is important to remember that the benefit you derive from a
new business venture may differ substantially from what the
accounting profession (guided by IRS rules) considers to be your
taxable earnings from the activity. Such accounting conventions
are a necessary part of the tax code, but may be misleading if
you rely only on them when trying to figure out the value to you
of changing the status quo.

For example, your business venture may bring *non-monetary*
benefits – such as greater job satisfaction or shorter commutes –
that have no impact on taxable income. Forgetting to consider
these non-monetary benefits could lead you to reject an option
that would represent a genuine improvement over the status quo.

Accounting conventions may also allow you to assign *existing*
costs to new activities – and thereby make the new ventures look
less profitable than they actually are. Suppose, for example, that
a new project requires you to set up a home office. If you can
satisfy a number of IRS criteria[2] you will generally be able to
treat some of your current spending on mortgage payments,
household maintenance, utilities, cleaning services, insurance,

etc. as the cost of doing business. However, even if you qualify for this "home office deduction" on your Federal income taxes, it is important to remember that these are *current* expenses that are essentially irrelevant to your decision concerning a new business venture. In particular, if you start to think of these current expenses as part of the direct cost of a *new* project, then the new venture would end up looking less profitable than it is actually likely to be.[3] You might even be misled into turning down worthwhile proposals – ones that would have helped you pay for at least some of your current expenses. Similar arguments can be made concerning administrative overhead and equipment costs.

In later chapters, we will return to the question of whether accounting conventions provide the most relevant measures of benefits and costs – and discuss how to avoid being misled by any discrepancies encountered.

KEY POINTS TO REMEMBER:

❑   Base your analysis on the *full* set of benefits and costs *directly* attributable to the project under consideration, even if this means basing your decision on something other than profit as defined by accounting conventions (and the tax authorities).

☙ ☙ ☙

TRY IT YOURSELF!

You now have enough information to analyze your own small scale manufacturing and retailing ventures. This section provides you with a set of template tables to get you started. In later chapters we will consider the problem of accounting for the cost of new facilities and capital equipment purchases or leases.

Evaluating a Manufacturing Venture:

For manufacturing ventures as small as the quilt-making project, the basic resources you need to consider are the production materials, general supplies and the opportunity cost of funds (if any) you have tied up in inventory. You can adapt Table 4-8 to help you estimate the potential earnings from such projects.

Table 4-7: Earnings from Manufacturing

Items Sold:	1	5	10	15	20
Revenue received					
less					
Production materials					
Other supplies					
Wholesale and other discounts (if any)					
Opportunity cost of funds invested					
Net earnings					
Hours spent					
Earnings per hour					

Making Quilted Wall-Hangings Once Again: Here's a different version of Scenario 1 for those of you who would like to try a ready-made example before venturing out on your own.

For the sake of argument, suppose that the craft show vendor described in Scenario 2 offered you a second option: making up to 10 quilted wall-hangings at a price of $150 each. From experience, you know that

- each hanging will take 6 hours to make;
- each hanging requires 3 yards of fabric;

- the fabric you wish to use is on sale for 25 percent off its regular price of $8.98 per yard;
- each hanging requires $6 worth of other materials; and
- you are paid quickly enough that you have no significant on-going investment in this project (and can therefore reasonably ignore the opportunity cost of your funds).

Using this information to fill in Table 4-7, you should find that your earnings per hour would be $20.63 for any time spent making wall-hangings.

Evaluating a Retail Venture:

If you undertake a small retailing venture, your major expenses will be the cost of your inventory, your rent and the opportunity cost of any funds you have invested in the project. You can adapt Table 4-8 to help you estimate your potential earnings from such activities.

Table 4-8: Earnings from a Retail Venture

Units Sold	1	5	10	15	20	25
Revenue Received						
less: Wholesale cost of inventory						
Shipping cost						
Rent						
Sales commissions, trade discounts, etc.						
Opp. cost of investment						
Total earnings						
Hours spent						
Earnings per hour						

Selling Framed Antique Tiles: Here's a different version of Scenario 2 for those of you who would like to try another ready-made example before venturing out on your own.

In one of the many catalogs that land in you mailbox, you notice that a craftsman is making frames designed to showcase the antique tiles that you are thinking about selling at the local antique mall. You know that

- tiles that are slightly fancier than the ones described in Scenario 3 will sell for $250 each if they are framed;
- your wholesale cost for these more elaborate designs is $110 per tile, with an additional $11 per tile needed for shipping and handling;
- the frames cost $75 each, including shipping and handling;
- the framed tiles would sell more readily in a larger showcase – one that rents for $30 a month, with the year's rent due in advance;
- the antique mall will require a 5 percent sales commission for this larger booth; and
- your opportunity cost of invested funds remains at 5 percent.

Using this information to fill in Table 4-8, you should find that you would earn roughly $16 per hour if you sold 24 tiles per year. (The precise answer will depend on how you compute the opportunity cost of your funds invested.)

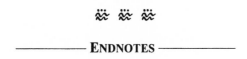

──────────── ENDNOTES ────────────

[1] It may also be helpful to note that the alternative set of answers ("No" to the first question and "Yes" to the second) has

a parallel interpretation. If you find that cost is *not* incurred if you go ahead with a venture ("No" to the first question) and *is* incurred if you continue the status quo ("Yes" to the second questions), then you will have identified a *benefit* of the new venture in the form of a cost avoided. Suppose for example that you are considering quitting a full-time office job and going into business for yourself. Suppose further that if you work for yourself, you will spend more time at the computer in your home office -- and less time sitting in rush hour traffic dressed in your business suit. Any resulting decrease in your car expenses and dry cleaning bills would be a direct benefit of the new venture, while any increase in your computer-related expenditures would be a direct cost.

[2] According to the IRS, in order to quality for a home office deduction, your use of the business part of your home must be *exclusive, regular, for your trade or business,* AND the business part of your home must be one of the following: your principal place of business OR a place where you meet or deal with customers in the normal course of your trade or business, or a separate structure you use in connection with your trade or business. IRS Publication 587, *Business Use of Your Home* provides more details on these criteria. This and other IRS publications are available on the IRS web site, www.irs.gov.

[3] In fact, just the opposite may be true. If the proposed project makes it possible to deduct a portion of your routine housing expenses from your taxable income, then the new project may provide a tax benefit even if it does not generate a substantial profit. However, given the complexity of the deduction criteria and the ensuing tax computations, you would be wise to consult an accountant as you work to sort out the tax implications of such your proposed home office.

5

Growing Your Business and Your Profits

In the last chapter, we tackled the question of whether or not you could at least break even – cover your opportunity costs – by going into business for yourself. Let's assume that you did decide to go ahead with the business venture you were considering. Once you have your business up and running, you will face a different set of issues. Two of the most basic questions are

- How should I serve my existing customers or clients?
- How many customers or clients do I ultimately want to have?

Business principles tell us that these questions are best answered in sequence. In other words, you first need to decide how you would work with different sets of customers if and when the need arises – and then determine how many customers you actually wish to attract. Business principles also provide the key to answering these questions. In this chapter you will see how to use concepts like "marginal revenue" and "marginal cost" to predict the results of your business decisions.

※ ※ ※

WHY MARGINAL?

Before we turn to specific cost and revenue measures, it is important to understand why we use the term "marginal" so often. The word itself is easy to translate: "marginal" is simply another way of saying "change in." Unfortunately, this translation does not really clarify the role that business analysts assign to the word "marginal". To see *why* the word is used, we must look at the basic logic of economic analysis.

Strip away the jargon and you will find that developing your business strategy is really an exercise in tinkering with the status quo. The fundamental question becomes, "What will happen if I...?" Whether you adjust your price, your production methods, or the mix of goods and services that you sell, you will always want to know how the proposed strategy affects your bottom line.

To answer this question, business analysts typically start by looking at cost and revenue separately. They then combine these observations to predict the impact of a proposed change on expected profit. Individual cost and revenue effects are labeled *marginal* because they indicate the expected result of a proposed change. In other words, the term *marginal* reminds us that we are looking at the aftermath of an adjustment – the impact on a particular financial measure of tinkering with the status quo. When *all* of the relevant marginal effects are taken together, they tell us what to expect if and when the proposed strategy is actually adopted.

In the sections that follow, you will find definitions of commonly-cited marginal effects, along with examples that show how to use these concepts when making business decisions.

Marginal and Incremental Cost

As you decide just how to meet the needs of different customers, you will need to figure out how to produce varying amounts of the goods and/or services you sell. To make these production choices, you will need to know how much it will cost you to meet the needs of current and potential customers.

The *additional* cost you incur as you expand production is generally known as the *marginal cost* of additional output. More precisely, *marginal cost is the added cost incurred when increasing production by a single unit.* In practice, it is often calculated from small changes in production volume: you divide the expected change in cost by the change in production volume.

To see how marginal cost would be measured in a simple example, let's assume for the moment that you are designing and producing decorative greeting cards for sale to local gift shops. Assembling each of the cards requires a variety of supplies: plain card stock and an envelope, glue and tape, bits of decorative paper and an embellishment such as a pewter or brass charm. The following table shows what you now pay for each of these supplies – the "inputs" needed for your production process.

Table 5-1: Greeting Card Supply Costs

Item:	Cost per Card
Card stock plus envelope	$.72
Decorative papers, glue, tape	$.50
Embellishment	$.25
Supply Cost per Card	$1.47

From Table 5-1 we see that your supply cost is $1.47 per card. You therefore expect your total supply cost to increase by $1.47 for each additional card that you make. In other words, your marginal supply cost is $1.47.

Your "full" marginal cost of producing an additional card would, of course, include the opportunity cost of the time you spend on this activity – both assembling individual cards and attending to administrative chores. Suppose, for example, that it took 10 minutes (1/6 of an hour) to assemble a card and record it as inventory. If the opportunity cost of your time was $18 per hour, then the full marginal cost of producing an additional card would be $4.47 – the sum of $1.47 for supplies and $18/6 or $3 for 10 minutes of your time. As we will see later, these *marginal* cost measures can be used to predict the impact on your total cost of expanding (or contracting) your business activities.

Incremental cost is a closely related concept, one that essentially broadens the notion of marginal cost to include larger or more general changes. Specifically, your incremental cost is defined as the change in cost attributable to a general change in policy, strategy or production volume. Unlike the marginal cost computations above, you do *not* divide by the expected change in the number of units. Instead, you simply compute the full impact of the proposed change on your costs. This effect can then be compared with the benefits traceable to the policy change in question. For example, the incremental cost of opening a new store or introducing a new product line would include new fixed costs (like added rent, design or licensing fees) as well as your regular production expenses (like your purchases of materials and the opportunity cost of your time).

KEY POINTS TO REMEMBER:

❑ **Marginal Cost** is defined as the cost of producing *one extra unit* of the good or service you sell.

❑ **Marginal Cost** is computed as a ratio of two changes:

$$MC = \left(\frac{\text{change in}}{\text{production cost}} \right) \div \left(\frac{\text{change in}}{\text{units produced}} \right)$$

❑ **Incremental Cost** is defined as the full change in costs attributable to a specific policy change.

Marginal and Incremental Revenue

The next step is to decide how much you think people are willing to pay for the goods and/or services you wish to sell.

This information will ultimately help you refine your pricing strategy (and your desired sales volume).

For example, you may have a contract with a retailer that guarantees you a specific price per unit (up to some maximum quantity). Or you may realize that you have to lower your asking price in order to increase the number of items you sell. In either case, you will generally take in more revenue as you sell more goods and services. This added revenue is often called *marginal revenue*: the extra revenue generated by extra units sold. By analogy with marginal cost, marginal revenue is computed by dividing the change in revenue by the change in units sold.

KEY POINT TO REMEMBER:

❑ **Marginal Revenue** is defined as the added revenue you earn from selling *one extra unit* of your good or service.

❑ **Marginal Revenue** is computed as a ratio of two changes:

$$MR = \left(\begin{array}{c} \text{change in} \\ \text{sales revenue} \end{array} \right) \div \left(\begin{array}{c} \text{change in number} \\ \text{of units sold} \end{array} \right)$$

❑ **Incremental Revenue** is defined as the added revenue received from the sale of multiple units of your good or service.

The Profit Objective of Business Owners

A quick glance at the business pages of your favorite newspaper will probably tell you more than you wanted to know about recent debates over measures of business *profit*. The notion of profit *is* central to economic and financial analysis:

entrepreneurs are almost always described as profit-maximizers. And probably as a result, we have an abundance of competing definitions of this objective.

The various definitions all share a common structure: profit is *always* defined as the difference between benefit and cost. However, this consensus breaks down when it comes to saying precisely *what* benefit and *which* costs. There is usually a good reason for this disagreement: the appropriate measures of benefit and cost will generally depend on the nature of the questions to be answered. For example, the tax authorities may treat your wage or labor income differently from your investment earnings even though both may be part of your general business activities as a sole proprietor.

The purpose of this book is to help you determine whether or not a business activity covers its *opportunity cost* – whether or not *your* benefit from the activity is greater than *your* cost. This question represents a core insight of economic or financial analysis; the answer provides the guidance necessary to make certain that your resources are used as effectively as possible.

Given this purpose, it makes sense to **define your profit objective as the benefit you receive over and above the opportunity cost of the time and money you devote to your business.** For example, if you have the chance to earn $100 in a new business venture and the your opportunity cost of the time required is $75, then your profit would be $25 by this definition. (The IRS would, of course, say that your business income is $100 and would want to tax you on the full amount.)

This definition of your profit objective helps you identify desirable business ventures: any project that earns a positive profit represents an improvement over the status quo used to define your opportunity cost.   Even if your profit from a new venture is as low as $5, you will be better off taking on the project: you will have covered the opportunity cost of your time with $5 to spare!

For the remainder of this book, we will analyze business opportunities in terms of their impact on this notion of your business profit.   We will generally define the benefit of a business venture as the revenue generated by the activity; the cost of a business venture will be assumed to include the full opportunity cost of the resources used, especially the value *to you* of the time devoted to the activity. Nevertheless, it is important to remember that this definition of your business objective is broad enough to include a variety of benefits and costs. The satisfaction you get from running your own business or even just having a more flexible work schedule simply become non-monetary benefits; whatever concerns you may have about the possible risks of such autonomy translate into non-monetary costs.

Lastly, we will assume that your goal is to maximize your profit – as we have just defined it – to derive as much value as possible from the resources at your disposal.

KEY POINTS TO REMEMBER:

❑ Your **profit objective** as a business owner is defined as the difference between the total benefit you receive from your business venture and the opportunity cost of all resources used in the activity – including the value of your time.

❑ Business owners are assumed to seek to maximize this notion of profit.

YOUR DESIRED SCALE OF OPERATION

By combining information about revenue – or consumer "willingness-to-pay" – with your cost analysis, you will be able to decide how many customers and clients you wish to attract. In general, there is a simple process for choosing the scale of your operations:

- continue to grow your business as long as the benefit you derive from the expansion is at least as great as the cost of the additional production.

A more concise version of this rule is found in many texts on business management:

- expand your business activities if marginal revenue is at least as great as marginal cost.

Although the words differ, the logic of these rules is the same. In fact, both guidelines are simply restatements of the opportunity cost principle we discussed in earlier chapters. In each case, the recommended strategy is to undertake all projects that cover their respective opportunity costs – taking as given whatever else you are already doing. For example, if you can expand production at a cost of $4 per item and sell this additional output for a few pennies more, it probably makes sense to do so – unless an even better option is available.

KEY POINTS TO REMEMBER:

To maximize your profit,

❑ expand your business as long as the *added* benefit from expansion covers the *added* cost, and

❑ scale back your business if you can save more in production cost than you will lose in sales revenue or other benefits.

In the remainder of this chapter, we use a simple manufacturing business to explore this principle in greater depth.

❄ ❄ ❄

THE COST OF EXPANDING PRODUCTION

If you have chosen to become a manufacturer, there are typically several ways to increase the number of items you can offer for sale. In most situations, you can either
- work longer hours, or
- contract with an outside professional to help you with administrative chores, or
- bring in someone to help you with production, or
- send partially-finished goods to an off-site contractor,

or use some combination of these options. Similar sets of options exist for retailers and professional service companies. In all likelihood, you will choose different alternatives as your business evolves and grows. In any case, the choices you make will determine the cost of additional output for your company.

Production Requirements

To see how this works in practice, consider a business similar to the quilt-making project discussed in Chapter 4. Let's assume that you are in the business of making quilted wall-hangings. You know that each wall-hanging requires three yards of fabric and $6 worth of other materials. The fabric you prefer to use usually costs $8.98 a yard, but is now on sale for 75 percent of its regular price. As a result, the fabric cost is $20.21 per quilt; the total out-of-pocket cost – fabric and other materials combined – is $26.21.

You know from experience that each wall-hanging takes 4 1/3 hours to produce; you also know that you need to allow 2/3 hour per quilt for administrative chores such as bookkeeping, shipping, purchasing, etc. You can either do these tasks yourself, or contract with someone to help with some or all of them.

Out-Sourcing Options

Before you decide to hire outside help, you first need to figure out how much it will cost you to do the task yourself. To do this you need to figure out the opportunity cost of your time – the value *to you* of the hours you will spend on this project. Let's assume that you have already done the analysis described in Chapters 2 and 3 and discovered from these calculations that the opportunity cost of your time is $15 per hour. (Remember that this amount reflects both the money you could have earned by taking a different job *and* the personal benefit to you of being your own boss.)

Given the nature and size of your business, there are two types of outside help available to you. You can contract with your accountant to assume most of your administrative duties at a cost of an additional $90 per week. Doing so will save you 4 1/3 hours per week – time that you can devote to production, leisure, or new business ventures. You also know that there are a few administrative chores that cannot be delegated; you expect these to take up roughly one hour per week.

Your other option is to "out-source" part of the production process. In other words, you can arrange for someone else to take over manufacturing tasks such as cutting, pattern piecing, final assembly, etc. After some consideration, you decide that you enjoy choosing fabric combinations, cutting out patterns and stitching the pieces together to form the wall-hanging design. On the other hand, you would be happy to delegate the task of final assembly to someone else if you could do so at a reasonable price. You know of a professional quilter who will assemble a wall-hanging for $35. For every three unfinished wall-hangings you send to this quilter, you save yourself 4 1/3 hours – time that you can spend on other aspects of your business.

Although the issue is easily resolved in this particular case, it is generally important to keep in mind the distinctions between contractors and employees recognized by the Internal Revenue Service. The difference between these categories of staff depends upon workplace conditions – the extent of worker independence

– rather than on individual job titles. According to the IRS,[1] the primary job attributes of interest are

- the extent of management control over staff behavior: the choice of location, equipment, types of supplies, job assignments, and task sequences;

- the extent of management control over the financial aspects of the job: the extent of unreimbursed business expenses, the worker's personal investment, the worker's exposure to risk, and the number of the worker's distinct clients; and

- the nature of the relationship between the worker and the client: the permanency of the relationship and whether or not the worker is paid benefits such as health insurance or paid holidays and sick leave.

For this quilting example, you can make a strong case that any outside help you are likely to hire would be classified as outside contractors. Both your accountant and the professional quilter would have a number of other clients besides you and would therefore not be your common law employees. However, other types of staff may imply other outcomes: the IRS may well consider an administrative assistant who worked for you on a part-time basis to be your employee.

The distinction between employees and contractors is important because a business has far more varied obligations to its employees. While a business may pay a contractor on a straight hourly rate – or a simple lump-sum fee for a specific project – the same company will generally have to pay its employees an agreed-upon wage plus a standardized set of benefits. As the IRS observes,

> [a]n employer must generally withhold income taxes, withhold and pay social security and Medicare taxes, and pay unemployment tax on Wages paid to an

employee. An employer does not generally have to withhold or pay any taxes on payments to independent contractors.[2]

As a rule, you need to make sure that you account for the full cost of any supplemental staff you hire. If you do choose to bring on employees, you can of course use an accountant or a payroll agencies assist with the administrative paperwork.

Production Costs

The next task is to determine when, if ever, it makes sense to use these various outside services. Table 5-2 shows how your costs vary as you change the number of wall-hangings you make each week. The table is based on the assumption that you choose to work no more than 40 hours per week and reflects the other production options described earlier.[3]

Table 5-2: Wall-Hanging Production Costs

Units per Week	Fabric	Other Material	Own Prod. Hours	Own Admin. Hours	Opp. Cost of Own Time
1	$20.21	$6	4 1/3	2/3	$75
2	$40.41	$12	8 2/3	1 1/3	$150
3	$60.62	$18	13	2	$225
4	$80.82	$24	17 1/3	2 2/3	$300
5	$101.03	$30	21 2/3	3 1/3	$375
6	$121.23	$36	26	4	$450
7	$141.44	$42	30 1/3	4 2/3	$525
8	$161.64	$48	34 2/3	5 1/3	$600
9	$181.85	$54	39	1	$600
10	$202.05	$60	39	1	$600
11	$222.26	$66	39	1	$600
12	$242.46	$72	39	1	$600
13	$262.67	$78	39	1	$600

Table 5-2: Wall-Hanging Production Costs (continued)

Units per Week	Extern. Admin.	Extern. Prod.	Total Cost	Marginal Cost
1			$101.21	$101.21
2			$202.41	$101.21
3			$303.62	$101.21
4			$404.82	$101.21
5			$506.03	$101.21
6			$607.23	$101.21
7			$708.44	$101.21
8			$809.64	$101.21
9	$90		$925.85	$116.21
10	$90	$105	$1,057.05	$131.21
11	$90	$210	$1,188.26	$131.21
12	$90	$315	$1,319.46	$131.21
13	$90	420	$1,450.67	$131.21

We can learn a great deal from this production cost analysis. In particular, we can determine

- the maximum number of wall-hangings you can make if you work alone;
- how many additional wall-hangings you can make if you delegate most administrative chores;
- how many additional wall-hangings you can make if you delegate most administrative chores and some production activities;
- how much money you will have to spend as the scale of your operations changes; and
- the total cost to you of this activity (including the opportunity cost of your time).

The First 8 Units: From the top half of the table, we see that you can make up to 8 wall-hangings per week by working strictly alone. For each one, you will have to spend $26.21 on fabric and other materials. You will also have to devote 5 hours of your own time to make the hanging and finish the related administrative tasks. In other words, each of the first 8 wall-hangings costs you $101.21: a total of $26.21 for materials and $75 for your own time. It follows that your *marginal cost* for wall-hangings is $101.21 – as long as you make no more than 8 of them.

The Ninth Unit: You know that you will need to find outside help if you want to expand production beyond 8 wall-hangings per week. You know that you need to free up 4 1/3 hours to manufacture the ninth wall-hanging. You can accomplish this by either contracting out virtually all administrative tasks or sending out three wall-hangings out to be assembled by a professional quilter. You know that the bill for the administrative help would be $90 per week, while the cost of having someone else assemble three wall hangings would be $105. Since you want to limit your out-of-pocket costs as much as possible, you choose to seek administrative help. As a result, the marginal cost of the ninth wall hanging rises to $116.21 – the amount you will have to spend on extra materials and administrative assistance. (Since the total amount of time *you* spend on the project remains constant at 40 hours per week, there is no change in the opportunity cost of your time.)

The Tenth Unit: If you wish to produce more than 9 wall-hangings per week, you have only one option left: spend less of your own time on final product assembly and more of your own time on initial cutting and stitching. You know that you can free up 4 1/3 hours – the time you need to produce an extra wall-hanging – for every 3 units you send out to be finished. Putting this trade-off into practice, we see that you must spend on $105 on external production help (*and* $90 on administrative expenses) in order to make 10 wall hangings. The marginal cost of the tenth unit is therefore $131.21 – the sum of all *additional* out-of-pocket costs.

Units 11, 12, and 13: You can expand production by three more units by sending out yet more wall-hangings for professional assembly. The marginal cost of each of these last two units is again $131.21 – the additional cost of materials and production help needed to manufacture each extra wall-hanging.

Once your weekly production volume has reached 13 units, you will face a different sort of capacity constraint. At this point, you will be cutting and stitching 13 wall-hangings per week. You will be sending 12 of these units out to be professionally finished, and will assemble the remaining one yourself. In order to expand production any further, you will have to change the nature of your involvement in your business and hire full-time staff to help you with initial cutting and stitching. As we see in the next section, the benefit of such continued expansion depends on how much revenue you receive for each wall-hanging you sell.

Other Opportunity Costs: It is important to remember that there is one potentially important resource cost missing from Table 5-2: the opportunity cost of the money you have invested in the business. The simplified structure of this example enables us to postpone consideration of this cost: since we assume that you already have the all of the equipment needed to manufacture wall-hangings, we do not have to account for the capital costs directly associated with this project. By assuming that you sell your products quickly, we can also avoid accounting for the cost of maintaining unsold inventory on hand. (We will change these assumptions in later examples and consider investment opportunity costs in somewhat greater detail.)

The time you spend on planning – or developing your market strategies – represents another cost of doing business that deserves consideration in some circumstances. If you are trying to decide how long to work on your business plan – or even the examples in this book – the opportunity cost of the time involved *is* a relevant cost of doing business. However, once you have settled on your planning strategy, the time spent reaching this conclusion is a sunk cost and no longer relevant to future decisions. You cannot change the past and do something else with the time!

~ ~ ~

THE BENEFIT OF EXPANDING PRODUCTION

At this point, we know both the method and the cost of meeting the needs of various numbers of customers. Table 5-2 indicates both *how* you would produce any given number of wall-hangings, and *how much* you would have to spend to do so. Nevertheless, we have yet to tackle the issue of just how many wall-hangings you actually *want* to make and sell.

Surprisingly enough, the answer is usually *not* "sell as many wall-hangings as possible." As we noted at the beginning of this chapter, the "ideal" company size (or production volume) depends on a comparison of the marginal benefits and costs of increased production. In general, making more wall-hangings – or any other saleable product or service – will increase your profit only if the extra revenue from additional sales is sufficient to cover the added cost of production. In other words, it pays to expand production as long as your marginal revenue is greater than your marginal cost.

In order to apply this "marginal cost approach" to the problem of deciding how many wall-hangings to make, you need information about consumer *demand* for this product. In particular, you need a sense of how much customers are willing to pay for a given number of items.

Selling at a Fixed Price: Let us assume for the moment that the owner of a local craft gallery likes your work and is willing to buy as many wall-hangings as you can make at a price of $126 each. At first, you might think that at this price it makes sense to produce as many as possible. After all, fabric and materials only cost $26.21 per hanging, and the average expense – apart from the cost of your own labor – of making 13 hangings per week is just over $65 per hanging. Nevertheless, more careful business judgement suggests a slightly different strategy, one based on a comparison of marginal revenue and marginal cost.

Consider first the revenue you receive from the sale of one extra wall-hanging. Under the terms of your agreement with the craft gallery owner, your marginal revenue is the same as the unit price offered: each wall-hanging you make and sell brings you $126 in extra revenue.

For information about your marginal cost, we turn to Table 5-2. As we mentioned earlier, the marginal cost of the first 8 items is $101.21 (including the opportunity cost of the time you spend). The marginal cost of the ninth unit is $116.21, and the marginal cost of each of the last 4 units is $131.21. Overall, we see that your marginal cost starts out low and increases as your production volume grows. This is a fairly common characteristic of production processes: at some point, it usually becomes increasingly difficult to make "just one more" widget.

We now have enough information to apply our marginal cost approach and choose a desired production volume. Table 5-3 summarizes our findings thus far and lays out the implications for your potential earnings from making wall-hangings. In each case, "total revenue" is equal to the price per wall-hanging times the number of units sold to the gallery operator. "Total Cost" is defined in Table 5-2 above as the full cost of production including the value of your time. "Earnings in Excess of Opportunity Cost" is the difference between your revenue and your total cost. Thus it represents the benefit you receive over and above the value to you of your next best option.

Table 5-3: Earnings from Wall-Hanging Sales

Units per Week	Total Revenue	Total Cost	Profit = Revenue *less* Cost	Marginal Revenue	Marginal Cost
1	$126	$101.21	$24.80	$126	$101.21
2	$252	$202.41	$49.59	$126	$101.21
3	$378	$303.62	$74.39	$126	$101.21
4	$504	$404.82	$99.18	$126	$101.21
5	$630	$506.03	$123.98	$126	$101.21
6	$756	$607.23	$148.77	$126	$101.21
7	$882	$708.44	$173.57	$126	$101.21
8	$1,008	$809.64	$198.36	$126	$101.21
9	*$1,134*	*$925.85*	*$208.16*	*$126*	*$116.21*
10	$1,260	$1,057.05	$202.95	$126	$131.21
11	$1,386	$1,188.26	$197.75	$126	$131.21
12	$1,512	$1,319.46	$192.54	$126	$131.21
13	$1,638	$1,450.67	$187.34	$126	$131.21

Since your time is scarce and valuable, you would like to use it well. Table 5-3 shows how you can use our marginal cost approach to find your preferred scale of operations. The process is simple: you must

- first choose a plausible production strategy; and
- then check to see if you can increase your earnings by adjusting it.

You need to repeat this thought process until no further gains are possible. At that point, you should have the best available production strategy – as long as your revenue and cost estimates are accurate.

For example, suppose you thought that producing as much as possible – 13 wall-hangings per week – was a plausible option. At this point you would be spending 40 hours per week on your business, covering the $600 opportunity cost of your time, and earning a profit of $187.34 in excess of this opportunity cost.

However, after a brief look at the last two columns of Table 5-3 you realize that the cost of making the 13th wall-hanging was greater than the amount you were paid for it. You quickly figure out that you could do better by producing *fewer* wall-hangings. If you only made 12 per week, your profit would rise from $187.34 to almost $193 per week (and you would still cover the opportunity cost of your time). Nevertheless, you soon notice that even at this new production level your marginal cost is still higher than your marginal revenue, so you repeat the process, and consider the advantages of cutting production further.

Your Ideal Strategy: As you continue to revise your production strategy, you find that you can maximize your profit from this business by making 9 wall-hangings per week. If you produce fewer than 9, you forego some of your potential earnings. If you produce more than 9, you spend more than you earn on the last few items sold. At the best feasible scale of operations in this example, you expect to earn $208.16 more per week than the opportunity cost of your time. In other words, you take home a total of $808.16 instead of the $600 you would get from your next best alternative.

This result – that you earn the highest profit by producing 9 wall-hangings per week – illustrates the marginal cost approach we described at the beginning of this chapter. As Table 5-3 shows, marginal cost to you is below marginal revenue for production levels at or below 9 units per week. In other words, each unit produced earns at least as much as it cost to produce "at the margin." However, expansion beyond 9 units per week pushes marginal cost *above* marginal revenue. In other words, the tenth unit costs more to produce than it generates in revenue – and profit falls if it is in fact produced. It follows that you should stop expanding at 9 units per week.

※ ※ ※

CHOOSING THE SCALE OF A SERVICE BUSINESS

These business principles can also be used by anyone managing a professional practice. Although lawyers, accountants, health care professionals, etc. do not have to worry about the cost of materials or maintaining an inventory, they still have to decide how to divide their time between administration, staff supervision, and providing services directly to clients. In the following example, we consider the questions that must be answered by a clinical psychologist who is considering expanding her practice by contracting with part-time associates.

Expansion Opportunities: Patricia is a psychologist who currently devotes 40 hours per week to her clinical practice. She is able to spend 30 hours per week with patients and uses the remaining 10 hours per week to take care of administrative details and keep up with developments in her profession. Patricia knows that she would need to hire another psychologist on a part-time basis if she decided to expand her practice. However, Patricia also knows that she will have to spend some time supervising anyone she hires.

To simplify the problem, we assume that Patricia can hire contractors in four-hour increments, i.e., we assume that she can bring in contractors for 4, 8, 12, or 16 hours per week. For every 4 hours of time provided by a contractor, Patricia will have to spend at least one additional hour on supervision. Since she only has 40 a week to devote to her business, this means that she will have to cut back a little on her own clinical practice.

Table 5-4 details the specific tradeoff she faces. If Patricia wishes to bring in contractors for 4 hours per week, she will have to spend 1 extra hour on staff supervision. This approach implies that she will spend a total of 11 hours per week on administrative tasks and will cut back her own clinical practice to 29 hours per week. If she hires contractors to provide 8 hours of clinical services a week, she will have to spend another hour on administration for a total of 12 hours per week – and will therefore have to cut her own time with patients back to 28 hours per week.

As Patricia's scale of contracting continues to expand, so too does her incremental supervisory cost. If she chooses to bring in contractors for more than 8 hours per week, she will have to spend 2 extra hours on administration for each 4 hour increase in weekly contractor time. As a result, if Patricia chooses to increase contractor services from 8 hours to 12 hours per week she will have to increase her administrative time from 12 to 14 hours per week. The same incremental change occurs if she increases contractor time from 12 hours to 16 hours per week.

Table 5-4: Scheduling Hours in a Clinical Psychology Practice

Total Clinical Hrs.	Own Clinical Hrs.	Own Admin. Hrs.	Other Clinical Hrs.
30	30	10	
33	29	11	4
36	28	12	8
38	26	14	12
40	24	16	16

Patricia can use marginal revenue and marginal cost measures to choose among these options. She expects to charge $160 for each hour-long session with a patient and she knows that she will have to pay her contractors $90 for each hour of clinical services they provide. This information enables Patricia to compute her anticipated total and incremental revenues, as well as the total and incremental cost of the services provided by her practice.

Table 5-5: Weekly Revenues and Staff Costs for a Clinical Psychology Practice

Total Clinical Hours	Total Revenue	Incremen. Revenue	Total Contractor Cost	Incremen. Cost	Net Earnings
30	$4,800		$0		$4,800
33	$5,280	$480	$360	$360	$4,920
36	$5,760	$480	$720	$360	$5,040
38	$6,080	$320	$1,080	$360	$5,000
40	$6,400	$320	$1,440	$360	$4,960

It is clear from Table 5-5 that expanding from 30 to 33 clinic hours per week will increase Patricia's income. Specifically, we see that her incremental revenue ($480) exceeds her incremental cost ($360), and that her net earnings from the practice rise from $4,800 to $4,920. Expansion to 36 hours per week increases her earnings yet again – incremental revenue still exceeds incremental cost at this level. However, further expansion does not add to her income. If she uses 12 hours of contractor services per week, the added revenue ($320) does not cover the added cost of the time ($360) and her net earnings fall from $5,040 to $5000. Once again, we see that it pays to expand only as long as marginal (or incremental) revenue exceeds marginal (or incremental) cost.

᠕᠕ ᠕᠕ ᠕᠕

THE PRINCIPLES IN PRACTICE: AVERAGE VERSUS MARGINAL COST

In the last two examples, the decision-makers were assumed to have a great deal of information about cost and production processes before they chose finalized their respective business plans. You may not always have such detailed information about your available options. Fortunately, a marginal cost approach can still provide useful guidance. In this section we look at several common-place examples to see how these principles can be applied in other contexts.

Bayou Bijoux:

Judith is a jewelry designer who owns and operates Bayou Bijoux, a retail store in New Orleans. She knows how much it costs to manufacture silver necklaces and she knows how much it costs to run her store each month. Her necklaces currently sell for $25 each. At this price, Judith is able to manufacture and sell 70 necklaces a month. She is now wondering whether or not it makes sense to try to expand her production and her sales volume.

As Judith looks at the reports from her accountant, she finds that her production costs vary with the number of necklaces created, while the cost of her shop is fairly stable from month to month. Her accountant has provided her with additional information about the *average cost* of her inventory by taking her total monthly cost and dividing by the number of units produced. Table 5-6 summarizes this part of the accountant's report.

Table 5-6: Average Costs at Bayou Bijoux

Units Produced	Average Cost
65	$10
70	$11
75	$12

Judith remembers hearing about marginal cost analysis sometime in the distant past and wonders how to use the information in Table 5-6 to make a business decision. She realizes that her first task is to calculate her own marginal cost by looking at changes in total cost. Table 5-7 presents the results of her analysis.

Table 5-7: Marginal Costs at Bayou Bijoux

Units Produced	Average Cost	Total Cost	Marginal Cost
65	$10	$10 x 65 = $650	
70	$11	$11 x 70 = $770	($770-$650)/5 = $24
75	$12	$12 x $75 =$900	($900-$770)/5 = $26

Judith knows that *total cost* is simply the product of average cost and the number of units produced. For example, if the average cost of producing 70 necklaces is $11, then the total cost of this production volume is $770.

Judith's *marginal cost* calculation is a little more involved. To compute the added cost of a single necklace, she divides the *change* in total cost by the *change* in the number of units produced. For example, when her production run increases from 70 to 75, her total cost rises by $130 and the number of units she produces rises by 5. The ratio of these two number – i.e., her marginal cost estimate – is $130/5 or $26.

These marginal cost calculations provide Judith with particularly useful information. She sees that her marginal cost increases as she expands production – she attributes this to the fact that her own time is limited. In order to produce more necklaces, Judith knows that she would have to hire additional staff – and spend time supervising them. In other words, Judith realizes that increasing administrative duties can make it more expensive for her to get the *last* unit out the door than it cost her *on average* for the production run considered as a whole.

Whether or not it makes good business sense to expand production will depend on what price Judith can get for the extra units sold. At her current price of $25, she would be better off staying at her current production volume. Even though this price is substantially higher than her average cost of $11 per necklace, she knows that it will be very expensive to expand. Table 5-7 indicates that increasing current production by 5 units will cost an extra $130 – or $26 per additional necklace. If these added units sell for only $25 apiece, Judith stands to lose $5 per month by expanding.

The results of such marginal cost analysis are not always so dismal. For example, Judith would probably come to a different conclusion if she were offered the chance to fill a "special order" for a client willing to pay more for necklaces that she could customize at a relatively low cost.

Tampopo Textiles:

Mariko is a graphic artist who owns and operates Tampopo Textiles, a company she created to market her custom-designed fabrics. While Mariko creates the designs and chooses the colors to be used in her wares, she "out-sources" the actual production of the printed bolts of cloth. As a result, her average cost per bolt of cloth falls as she increases the size of a given production run.

Mariko's current production runs of printed silk are 500 bolts each; she now sells all of this fabric to a national retailer at a wholesale price of $22 a bolt. A local discount fabric store has expressed an interest one of her designs, but is only willing to pay $15 per bolt for a one-time order of 250 bolts. Mariko asked her accountant to estimate the impact of this added production her operating costs. Table 5-8 summarizes the results of this analysis.

Table 5-8: Average Cost of Fabric at Tampopo Textiles

Bolts Produced	Average Cost
500	$20
750	$16

Although $15 per bolt is below her average cost, Mariko suspects that this one-time order will still bring in enough revenue to cover its costs. To determine whether or not her intuition is correct, Mariko first computes the marginal cost of the additional bolts and then compares it to price offered.

Table 5-9: Marginal Cost of Fabric at Tampopo Textiles

Bolts Produced	Average Cost	Total Cost	Marginal Cost
500	$20	$10,000	
750	$16	$12,000	($12,000-$10,000)/250 = $8

Table 5-9 presents Mariko's results. After doing the math, she discovers finds that it only costs her $8 a bolt to make the extra fabric. As a result, she is inclined to accept the new order for $15 a bolt, with the understanding that this contract represents a discount for a new customer.

Megan's Muffins:

Megan is an innovative baker who sells breakfast muffins to a variety of local delis in Minneapolis. She currently sells 500 dozen muffins a week on a wholesale basis for $5 a dozen. Her current operating cost is $2000 per week; if she expands production by 10 percent, she knows that her operating cost will rise by 11 percent. Nevertheless, Megan suspects that expansion will add to her profits even though it increases her average cost.

To test her intuition, Megan computes the marginal cost of the extra muffins. She knows that after a 10 percent increase in production volume, she would have 500 x 1.1 = 550 dozen muffins to sell. She also knows that an 11 percent increase in cost means that her operating cost will be $2000 x 1.11 = $2,220 per week if she expands production.

Table 5-10: Marginal Cost at Megan's Muffins

Muffins Produced (dozen)	Operating Cost	Marginal Cost (per dozen muffins)
500	$2,000	
550	$2,220	($2,220 - $2,000)/(550-500) = $4.40

Table 5-10 presents Megan's marginal cost calculations. She realizes that it will cost her $220 more to produce an extra 50 dozen muffins each week. This translates into an added cost of $4.40 per dozen *new* muffins. Since this is less than her current wholesale price of $5 per dozen, she decides to look for additional customers who would be willing to pay this price.

≋ ≋ ≋

LESSONS LEARNED

Taken together, these examples illustrate one of the most important business insights to be gleaned from economics. Specifically, a project boosts your earnings if the added revenue it brings more than offsets the added cost of the activity The insight also works in reverse: a project hurts your bottom line if it costs more than it generates in revenue. In such a situation, it makes sense to consider abandoning the project – or perhaps savoring it simply for its non-monetary rewards.

In all of these cases, it is important to focus on the components of cost and revenue that actually *change*. Things that do not depend on the issue at hand – like non-refundable deposits, business leases, and other fixed expenses – are not directly relevant to your decision. For example, your choice of production volume does not generally depend on your monthly rent – unless the change contemplated would require you to rent more space than you currently have. The amount you pay in rent *will* affect your average cost of production and the amount of profit you earn. In other words, it will have a direct impact on your decision to enter a given market and stay there. However, once you have decided to operate a particular business, you need to pay strict attention to *marginal* costs and benefits in order to keep your bottom line as healthy as possible.

≋ ≋ ≋

TRY IT YOURSELF!

Applying these principles is a three-stage process. You must first identify the alternatives you wish to consider and their respective costs for different levels of activity. This information will enable you to compute the marginal or incremental cost of proposed changes.

The basic structure of Table 5-2 and Table 5-4 can be used as a template for your own analysis. Table 5-11 provides the outline of this breakdown of costs. The separate columns allow you to track your changing responsibilities as your volume of production evolves.

Table 5-11: Your Production Options

Units per Week	Direct Material Costs	Own Production Hours	Outsourced Production Expenses	Admin. Material Costs
1				
2				
3				
4				
5				
6				
7				
8				
9				
10				
11				
12				
13				

Table 5-11 (continued)

Units per Week	Own Administrative Hours	Other Administrative Expenses	Total Expenses	Marginal Expense
1				
2				
3				
4				
5				
6				
7				
8				
9				
10				
11				
12				
13				

The basic structure of Table 5-3 and Table 5-5 provides a template for the remainder of your analysis. The distinct columns in Table 5-12 will enable you to compare your price and marginal cost estimates directly, thereby finding the most profitable alternative.

Table 5-12: Earnings from Your Business

Units per Week	Price per Unit	Total Revenue	Total Project Cost	Marginal Cost	Project Earnings
1					
2					
3					
4					
5					
6					
7					
8					
9					
10					
11					
12					
13					

——————— ENDNOTES ———————

[1] See IRS publication 15-A, *Employer's Supplemental Tax Guide* (revised January 2002) for more information on this issue.

[2] Ibid., p. 5.

[3] This example is essentially unchanged if you are willing to consider working more than 40 hours per week: it is only necessary to increase the maximum number of wall-hangings that you can make without hiring outside help.

6

Pricing Your Goods and Services

As you learn more about the demand for the goods or services you sell, you will want to review your initial pricing and production decisions. Local gentrification or a down-turn in the regional economy may indicate that it is time to revise your prices or adjust the mix of things that you sell. National trends in consumer taste and changes in the number of your local competitors may also give you the incentive to review your marketing approach. Once again, marginal revenue and marginal cost concepts can help you refine your business strategies.

The basic rule remains the same as before – any change that increases your revenue more than it increases your cost will improve your "bottom line." In other words, we are still using marginal revenue and marginal cost concepts to evaluate our options – to see if it makes sense to tinker with the status quo. In the last chapter, we relied on a fairly simple pricing strategy: we treated the current asking price of goods (or services) as fixed. This approach allowed us to tackle a relatively simple question: "How much do we want to sell at this particular price?"

Reality is generally a bit more complicated. You will often suspect that you could sell a bit more, but only if you cut your prices. However, you also worry that the revenue gained from new sales will not make up for the revenue lost from existing customers once the price cut is in place. In this chapter, we examine a number of such marketing decisions. We start with a general example to establish the logic of the recommended strategy. We then develop several more focussed applications to illustrate how this approach can be adapted to a variety of situations.

≋   ≋   ≋

SELLING MORE AT A LOWER PRICE

To begin, let us suppose that you are trying to decide whether or not to work as a distributor for a friend who designs gold jewelry. You think that her gold earrings would sell well at the annual craft fair sponsored by the local college. However, before you offer to rent a booth and sell the jewelry your friend makes, you want to figure out whether or not the project makes good business sense. To do this, you will need information about

- the "wholesale price" you would need to pay for your inventory (i.e., the amount your friend would expect to receive for each item you sell);
- the fees charged by the college for having a booth at the craft fair;
- the cost of creating displays;
- the opportunity cost of your time, including setting up your booth before the fair opens and getting everything back home once the fair has ended;
- the number of items you can expect to sell at a given retail price – the results of your market research; and
- the extent of your responsibility if any of your merchandise is stolen.

Your Business Costs

To see how you can use this information to develop a

marketing strategy, we first look at your cost of doing business in this situation. We then examine the implications of your market research and recommend a pricing policy for this scenario.

Your Cost of Inventory: Let's assume that your friend has asked you to pay her $130 for each pair of earrings sold. She has also offered to take back any inventory that remains unsold at the end of the fair. In this situation, you only pay for the items that you actually sell. As a result, your total cost rises by exactly $130 every time you sell another pair of earrings. More formally, your marginal cost of inventory is $130 per pair of earrings.

The Opportunity Cost of Your Time: For this initial example, let's assume that your opportunity cost of spending a Saturday minding a booth at a craft fair is $15 per hour. As discussed in earlier chapters, this cost reflects the value to *you* of the next best use of your time, whether it be reading a novel, taking a part-time job, or doing volunteer work for the community. If you decide to participate in the fair, you expect to spend a total of 12 hours on the project (including travel time). As a result, the total opportunity cost of your time amounts to $15 x 12 = $180.

Other Costs of Doing Business: The craft fair organizers know that each year a large number of exhibitors will apply to enter the annual holiday show. To cover the cost of running the fair – and to contribute a little to the school's endowment – the college charges each exhibitor a non-refundable fee of $400 for booth space while the fair is open.

There are several other fixed expenditures associated with participating in this craft fair. You know that you will have to spend $150 to rent display cases and other furniture for your booth. You also expect to spend $120 on travel expenses (a hotel room, the added cost of restaurant meals, and gas for your van). As a result, your total out-of-pocket expenditures for participating in the craft fair amount to $400+$150+$120=$670.

Your Total Expenditures: By combining information about inventory costs, the opportunity cost of your time and various fixed costs, you can predict your total cost of participating in the craft fair. You know you have to cover out-of-pocket expenditures of $670 (plus your inventory cost of $130 per item) before you earn anything for the time devoted to this project. In order to cover the full opportunity cost of your time, you will have to earn an additional $180 over and above your out-of-pocket expenditures. In other words, your total fixed cost for this project amounts to $180+$670=$850.

Table 6-1 summarizes the results of these calculations. Your inventory cost for the craft fair is found by multiplying your cost per unit by the number of units you have on hand. Your total cost is calculated as the sum of your inventory cost, your opportunity cost and your various fixed costs.

Table 6-1: The Cost of Craft Fair Participation

Inventory on Hand	Cost per Unit (Marginal Cost)	Total Inventory Cost	Opportunity Cost of Time, Entrance Fee and Other Fixed Costs	Total Cost
5	$130	$650	$850	$1,500
8	$130	$1,040	$850	$1,890
11	$130	$1,430	$850	$2,280
14	$130	$1,820	$850	$2,670
17	$130	$2,210	$850	$3,060
20	$130	$2,600	$850	$3,450

Your Potential Customer Base

From past visits to this and similar fairs, you have a pretty good idea of the range prices charged for earrings like the ones your friend designs. From conversations with other craft jewelry dealers, you know that a lower price for a particular product typically translates into more units sold. The first two columns of Table 6-2 summarize the results of your market research:

they indicates just how many pairs of handmade gold earrings you can expect to sell at a number of different prices.[1] For example, according to your research summarized in the table you can expect to sell 11 pairs of earrings if you charge $250 per pair.

Table 6-2: Demand for Earrings at a Craft Fair

Asking Price	Expected Quantity Sold	Total Expected Revenue	Expected Marginal Revenue
$300	5	$1,500	
$275	8	$2,200	$233
$250	11	$2,750	$183
$225	14	$3,150	$133
$200	17	$3,400	$83
$175	20	$3,500	$33

Total Revenue from Sales: The price and quantity data you obtain from market research make it possible to work out your expected sales revenue and the corresponding expected marginal revenue per unit sold. The last two columns of Table 6-2 provide this analysis for the college craft fair.

Your "Total Expected Revenue" in the third column of Table 6-2 is simply the asking price multiplied by the expected quantity sold. For example, if your market research for the craft fair is accurate, you can expect to sell 8 pairs of earrings when you charge $275 per pair. At this price you expect to collect $275 x 8 = $2,200 in sales revenue. If you lower your price to $250 per pair of earrings, you expect to sell 11 pairs and generate $2,750 in sales.

Marginal Revenue from Sales: By lowering your price from $275 to $250, you expect to sell 3 additional pairs of earrings. However, these additional sales will *not* gain you $250 x 3 = $750 in additional revenue: the price cut will also cost you $25 on each of the 8 pairs of earrings you could have sold at a price of $275. Our definition of *marginal revenue* takes both the gains and the losses into account. To use the definition of marginal revenue given earlier,

- Compute the *change* in total sales revenue after a price change. For example, when you lower your price from $275 to $250, the change in your total revenue is $2,750 - $2,200 = $550.

- Compute the *change* in the number of units sold. When you lower your price from $275 to $250, the change in the number of units you sell is 11 - 8 = 3.

- Divide the change in your revenue by the change in your quantity sold to compute your marginal revenue. Specifically, $550/8 = $183 is your marginal revenue for the units sold as a result of lowering your price from $275 to $250.

The fourth column of Table 6-2 reports this marginal revenue measure for the full range of prices under consideration.

KEY POINTS TO REMEMBER:

❑ As before, *marginal revenue* is computed as a ratio of two changes:

$$MR = \left(\begin{array}{c} \text{change in} \\ \text{sales revenue} \end{array} \right) \div \left(\begin{array}{c} \text{change in number} \\ \text{of units sold} \end{array} \right)$$

❑ If you have to lower the price you charge existing customers in order to attract new business, then your *marginal revenue* will be less than your price: the revenue lost from existing customers will offset at least some of the revenue gained on new sales.

Recommended Pricing Strategy

What price should you actually charge? The answer depends primarily on your marginal revenue *and* what *you* have to pay for the things that you sell. In previous examples we found that it made sense to expand as long as the proposed change brought in enough revenue to cover any cost increases – i.e., as long as marginal revenue exceeded marginal cost. The same logic applies here.

Your Best Guess: A Starting Point: To see how this approach works in our craft fair example, start with your best guess about the price you should charge. Let's suppose that $250 sounds to you like a sensible retail price for a pair of gold earrings.

Now, calculate your expected cost and sales revenue for this choice. Given our previous assumptions about consumer demand and operating costs, your computations indicate that at a price of $250, you expect to sell 11 pairs of earrings at the craft fair, collect $2,750 in revenue and incur a total of $1,780 in operating expenses.

To see if you can improve upon this outcome, ask yourself the following questions:

- What will happen to my sales volume, revenue and operating costs if I *reduce* my asking price?
- What will happen to my sales volume, revenue and operating costs if I *raise* my asking price?

Your answers to these questions will provide you with the guidance you need to update your pricing strategy. Table 6-3 summarizes the answers implied by our initial assumptions about cost (Table 6-1) and sales revenue (Table 6-2). As Table 6-3 shows, you do expect to sell more pairs of earrings (and incur higher inventory costs) as you lower your price. However, the table also shows how the balance between marginal revenue and marginal cost shifts as your sales volume grows.

Table 6-3: Revenues and Costs at a Craft Fair

Asking Price	Expected Units Sold	Expected Total Sales Revenue	Expected Marginal Sales Revenue	Expected Total Cost (incl. Opp. Cost of Time)	Marginal Cost
$300	5	$1,500		$1,500	$130
$275	8	$2,200	$233	$1,890	$130
$250	11	$2,750	$183	$2,280	$130
$225	14	$3,150	$133	$2,670	$130
$200	17	$3,400	$83	$3,060	$130
$175	20	$3,500	$33	$3,450	$130

For example, if you *lower* your price from $250 to $225, you can expect to sell 3 more pairs of earrings at the fair, collect an additional $400 in sales revenue and spend an additional $390 on operating expenses. This translates into an expected marginal revenue of $133 and a marginal cost of $130 for each of the 3 new pairs of earrings sold.

The Best Bottom Line: The marginal cost approach described earlier suggests that you will be able to improve your bottom line by lowering your asking price and increasing the number of units you sell *as long as your marginal revenue is greater than your marginal cost of inventory*. Table 6-4 confirms this intuition.

Table 6-4: Profits from a Craft Fair

Asking Price	Expected Units Sold	Expected Marginal Revenue	Marginal Cost	Earnings in Excess of Opportunity Cost
$300	5		$130	$0
$275	8	$233	$130	$310
$250	11	$183	$130	$470
$225	*14*	*$133*	*$130*	*$480*
$200	17	$83	$130	$340
$175	20	$33	$130	$50

Your profit is highest when your asking price is $225 – the lowest price at which your marginal revenue exceeds your marginal cost. There is a good reason for this: if you lower your price below $225, you do not gain enough in revenue to cover your additional cost of inventory. And if you tried raising your price, you would lose more in revenue than you would save in inventory cost. Since we have eliminated the alternatives, an asking price of $225 becomes the best available option – assuming that your initial information was accurate.

KEY POINTS TO REMEMBER:

As before, to maximize your profit you should

❑   expand your business as long as the added benefit from expansion covers the added cost, and

❑   scale back your business if you can save more in production cost than you will lose in sales revenue.

❧ ❧ ❧

PRICING STRATEGIES TO AVOID

The craft fair example discussed in the previous section can also help us identify strategies that would *hurt* the bottom line of your business.

Maximizing Sales Revenue: Table 6-3 and Table 6-4 illustrate the negative impact on profits of trying to earn as much *revenue* as possible. On the basis of the information you have before the craft fair begins, you realize that maximizing your expected sales revenue would mean lowering your asking price to $175 per pair of earrings.   At this price, you would expect to generate $3,500 in sales revenue. However, you would expect to earn only $50 in profit, an amount that represents a loss of $430 relative to your profit-maximizing strategy.

As mentioned earlier, our marginal cost approach provides a ready explanation for this loss: the last six pairs of earrings sold did not cover their marginal cost. If you increased your price to $200, you would sell 3 fewer pairs of earrings, but you would lose only $100 in revenue: the price increase helps offset the smaller sales volume. It follows that the marginal revenue per unit for these last three pairs was $100/3 or $33.33. However, under the terms of your agreement with the friend who made the earrings, you owe her $130 per pair. As a result, you would lose almost $97 in profit on each of the last three pairs sold. Fortunately, you can avoid this loss by simply raising your price to $200.

The same argument can be made for raising your price to $225 instead of leaving it at $200. If you were to raise your price by another $25 you would again sell 3 fewer pairs of earrings. However, you would only lose $250 in revenue. It follows that the marginal revenue for each of these pairs was $250/3 or $83.33. Since the marginal cost of these items would again be $130, you would lose roughly $47 in earnings on each of these pairs. Once more, you can avoid this loss by raising your price to $225 – the lowest price at which marginal revenue exceeds marginal cost.

KEY POINTS TO REMEMBER:

❑   If you try to maximize your *sales revenue*, you will
    usually end up setting your price *too low* to
    maximize your profit: the revenue you gain from
    the last item sold is likely to be less than its
    marginal cost.

❑   If your marginal revenue is in fact less than your
    marginal cost, you can increase your profit by
    raising your price and scaling back production.

Concern over Fixed Costs: Although fixed costs – such as
entrance fees or set-up costs – do influence your decision about
participating a given craft fair, the level of these costs (all else
being equal) should not affect your pricing decisions once you
have decided which fairs to attend. Our marginal cost approach
provides a quick explanation for this result: since your fixed
costs do not vary with changes in your sales volume, they do not
enter into your pricing strategy analysis.

To put this insight into practice, consider several alternate
versions of our earlier craft fair example. We saw earlier that if
the college sponsoring the craft fair charged you an entrance fee
of $400, then your expected profit was the highest when you set
a price of $225 per pair of earrings. At this price you expected
to sell 14 pairs and earn a net profit of $480 from this particular
craft fair.

Table 6-5 shows the impact on your earnings of changes in
the craft fair entrance fee. The last two columns of this table are
computed using the same revenue and marginal cost assumptions
as found in Table 6-4; only the craft fair participation fees – a
major component of your fixed costs – are different.

Table 6-5: Profits from a Craft Fair Revisited

Asking Price	Expected Units Sold	Expected Marginal Revenue	Marginal Cost	Earnings in Excess of Opp. Cost, Fee = $100	Earnings in Excess of Opp. Cost, Fee = $700
$300	5		$130	$300	-$300
$275	8	$233	$130	$610	$10
$250	11	$183	$130	$770	$170
$225	*14*	*$133*	*$130*	*$780*	*$180*
$200	17	$83	$130	$640	$40
$175	20	$33	$130	$350	-$250

From Table 6-5 we see that your optimal pricing strategy remains *unchanged* even if the college lowers its participation fee to $100 or raises it to $700. Since the change in the participation fee does not affect your marginal cost, a retail price of $225 remains your highest-profit option.

This observation does not imply that your profits are immune from changes in the cost of entering the craft fair. Quite the opposite: a $100 change in the entrance fee translates directly into a $100 change in your earnings.

Such changes in fixed costs can influence your decision to attend the fair. If, for example, the entrance fee rose from $400 to $700 and your travel costs rose from $120 to $320, then you would never be able to cover the cost of participating in the fair. Nevertheless, as long as the entrance fee is low enough to make it worth you while to participate, your pricing strategy will not be influenced by the level of the entrance fee – all else being equal.

KEY POINTS TO REMEMBER:

❑ Although *fixed costs* – or costs that do not change
   when you make small adjustments in your scale of
   operations – do affect your profit, they do *not* influence
   your profit-maximizing pricing strategy.

❑ Once you have decided to enter a particular market,
   you need only consider *marginal costs* when choosing
   your pricing strategy.

༄ ༄ ༄

THE PRINCIPLES IN PRACTICE: MORE PRICING EXAMPLES

In some situations, you may have relatively limited market
information available when you need to make pricing decisions.
In this section, we look at several less-detailed examples to see
how to apply a marginal cost approach in such circumstances.

Millie's Muffins

Millie owns and operates the only bakery in a small town. It
is unlikely that anyone else will open a competing muffin shop.
The shop currently sells 400 muffins a day at a retail price of
$1.10 each. If Millie lowered her price to $1.00, she would
expect to sell 460 muffins each day. Given her current level of
production, Millie's marginal cost of 60 extra muffins is $.25 per
muffin.
    What option would you advise Millie to choose?   This
question can be tackled using our marginal cost approach. To do
so, we must first estimate Millie's marginal revenue and then
compare it to her marginal cost.

Table 6-6: Marginal Revenue, Millie's Muffins

Price	Quantity	Revenue	Marginal Revenue
$1.10	400	$440	
$1.00	460	$460	$0.33

We see from Table 6-6 that Millie earns a marginal revenue of $20/60 = $.33 per muffin for the extra 60 muffins she sells if she lowers her price to $1.00. Given her current market information, this marginal revenue exceeds her marginal cost. As a result, lowering her price will improve her bottom line as long as her information proves correct.

If a price cut leads to a smaller change in her sales volume, Millie may prefer to leave her retail price at $1.10. Suppose, for example, that lowering her price to $1.00 only increases Millie's sales by 50 muffins per day.

Table 6-7: Marginal Revenue, Millie's Muffins Revisited

Price	Quantity	Revenue	Marginal Revenue
$1.10	400	$440	
$1.00	450	$450	$0.20

We see from Table 6-7 that in these circumstances, a $.10 price cut implies a marginal revenue of $10/50 = $.20 per muffin. Since this amount is less than her current marginal revenue of $.25, Millie would be well advised to avoid this change in her pricing strategy.

Tanya's Tweeds

Tanya owns and operates a clothing store selling imported woolens. She currently carries a line of sweaters with a recommended retail price of $200. At this price she expects to sell 100 sweaters each season. Tanya believes that she will sell 5 more sweaters if she reduces her price by $5. Table 6-8 details the revenue implications of this scenario.

Table 6-8: Marginal Revenue for Tanya's Tweeds

Price	Quantity	Revenue	Marginal Revenue
$200	100	$20,000	
$195	105	$20,475	$95

For what range of wholesale costs does it make sense for Tanya to lower her retail price to $195? Our marginal cost approach can help us tackle this question. As long as Tanya's cost of an additional sweater is less than $95, the price cut is likely to improve her bottom line: her marginal revenue per sweater ($95 for the last 5 sweaters sold) will exceed her marginal (i.e., her wholesale) cost.

≈≈ ≈≈ ≈≈

LESSONS LEARNED

We have now looked a number of situations in which it makes sense to tinker with the status quo. In each case, we saw that if your expected revenue rose by *more* than your cost when your sales volume grew, then it would pay to *lower* your asking price – and sell more of your product or service. Conversely, if your expected revenue rose by *less* than your cost in these circumstances, then it would pay to consider *raising* your asking price and selling less of your product or service.

This approach – analyzing possible tradeoffs between added revenue and added cost – can be adapted to help a wide variety of puzzles. You can tackle virtually any business decision this way – including

- **the variety of products you plan to sell;**
- **the pricing strategy you plan to use** (when to have sales, when to offer discounts, whether or not to introduce a frequent buyers' club, etc.);
- **the types of markets you plan to enter** (and how many of each type) – wholesale, retail, mail order, intermittent trade show or craft fair, etc.;
- **your marketing strategy** – by direct mail or by advertisements in the local newspaper, the Yellow Pages or regional theater Playbills; via the Web or in special interest magazines or trade journals;
- **how many full-time employees to hire;**
- **how many consultants to retain on contract;**
- **when to purchase new equipment;** or even
- **when to move to a new location.**

In each case, you need to determine the impact of the proposed change on both your costs and your revenue. If the added benefits exceed the added costs, then the change is probably a good idea!

In the final section of this chapter, you will find templates designed to help you gather the information you need to analyze your own situation in terms of marginal cost and marginal revenue. In the next chapter, we will see how this approach can also help you identify the information you *don't* need – misleading information that could induce you to reject profitable opportunities.

≈ ≈ ≈

TRY IT YOURSELF!

Table 6-9 is essentially a more general version of Table 5-11 presented at the end of the previous chapter.

Table 6-9: The Cost of Your Available Options

Scenario	Direct Material Costs	Cost of Outsourced Activities	Own Prod. Hours	Own Admin. Hours	Admin. Material Costs
Status Quo					
Alternative #1					
Alternative #2					
Alternative #3					
Alternative #4					
Alternative #5					
Alternative #5					

Table 6-9: The Cost of Your Available Options (continued)

Scenario	Other Fixed Costs	Total Cost	Incremental Cost
Status Quo			
Alternative #1			
Alternative #2			
Alternative #3			
Alternative #4			
Alternative #5			
Alternative #5			

The distinct columns in Table 6-10 will enable you to compare your price and marginal cost estimates directly, thereby finding the most profitable alternative.

Table 6-10: Earnings from Feasible Alternatives

Scenario	Price per Unit	Total Revenue	Total Project Cost	Incremental Cost	Project Earnings
Status Quo					
Alternative #1					
Alternative #2					
Alternative #3					
Alternative #4					
Alternative #5					
Alternative #6					

≋ ≋ ≋

———————— ENDNOTES ————————

[1] For the sake of simplicity in this example, assume that you choose a single retail price for the duration of the craft fair. We will tackle questions of quantity and to-the-trade discounts later, along with your incentive to change your price while the craft fair is in session.

7

Asking the Right Question

At this point, you have seen two fundamental economic concepts – opportunity cost and marginal analysis – used to solve common business problems. In your own business or professional life, you will face situations that are similar in structure even as they reflect the details and quirks of your own circumstances. The general approach recommended in this book – using the analysis of small feasible changes to make business decisions – can help you choose the opportunity that is right for you. From now on, your task is to figure out how to adapt this approach to suit you own needs.

One of the most useful aspects of this type of analysis is that it can help you ask the *right* questions – the ones that accurately reflect *your* interests. The examples presented in this chapter are designed to illustrate the importance of framing your questions carefully by showing what may happen when you fail to do so. In each of the cases discussed, opportunity cost considerations and/or the use of marginal analysis help clarify the nature of the problem at hand. As a result, it becomes easier to identify the best option for the business in question.

As before, the common element in these cases is an emphasis on the impact of *change*. The specific questions are similar to those asked in earlier chapters:

- Should I lower my price to attract more customers or clients?

- Will changing the mix of goods and services that I sell increase my earnings?

However, the discussion of the examples in this chapter emphasizes how *failing* to use opportunity cost and marginal analysis can actually hurt your business. Or, at a minimum, lead you to accept something other than the best of your available outcomes.

The first example in this chapter is similar to the craft fair example presented in Chapter 6. The difference here is that you now have the chance to adapt to new information *after* you have made an initial decision about participating in the fair. This example is designed to illustrate the importance of looking only at the choices yet to be made – and ignoring irrevocable decisions made in the past.

The second example shows the importance of distinguishing between average and marginal cost. Specifically, it reveals how offering a discount targeted to a well-defined group of customers can improve your "bottom line" even though the price charged appears to be "below cost."

The third example in this chapter again demonstrates the importance of focusing on marginal – rather than average – cost. In particular, it shows how common accounting conventions used to define the *average* cost of products or services may provide misleading information on the relative profitability of these items.   In other words, the example shows how conventions used to define average cost may lead you to ignore opportunities that actually improve your bottom line.

$$\approx \quad \approx \quad \approx$$

USING THE BEST AVAILABLE INFORMATION

As you learn more about your customers and your costs, you will probably want to revise and update your business plan in light of new information. You may find that your original choices of production techniques, sales volume or product price are no longer appropriate. With its emphasis on the *future* consequences of current decisions, opportunity cost reasoning and marginal analysis can help you identify the facts you need to keep your business on track and to make the most of the options you currently have at your disposal. The decisions to be made by the owner of a small business show how this forward-looking approach works in practice.

In the following case, the owner of a craft business faces two sets of questions: an initial decision on whether or not to register and prepare to be an exhibitor at an up-coming craft fair, as well as a later decision – on the actual day of the fair – on whether to go ahead with the original plan. In each case, opportunity cost reasoning helps the business owner tackle unresolved issues using the best available information.

To analyze the initial set of questions, we start by estimating total cost, including the opportunity cost of time. We then use this basic production information to determine the *marginal opportunity cost* of the crafts to be sold. The next step is to estimate how much consumers are willing to pay for the items this company produces. This marketing information is then used to calculate the *expected marginal revenue* from additional sales. By combining information about marginal revenue and marginal cost, the craft business owner can develop an initial strategy – an initial decision about whether or not to register, how much inventory to produce and how much to charge for the items to be sold at the fair.

On the day of the fair itself, new information may force the craft business owner to reconsider her initial decision about participating in the craft fair. As before, business principles indicate that such decisions should be made on the basis of *current* opportunity costs. In this case, the new set of issues is analyzed in terms of updated information on both expected marginal revenue and expected marginal cost.

Your Total Cost of an Activity:

Let's suppose that you make and sell designer gift cards at regional craft shows – a business venture that grew out of a hobby. You know that a craft show in a neighboring town has a low, but non-refundable, entrance fee – the show organizers charge each exhibitor $50 to participate. Since the show is so close to home, you know that there would be no extra travel costs associated this fair. You also realize that you could produce cards using designs that have sold well in the past. Nevertheless, you have not yet decided whether or not to participate in this particular show. Opportunity cost reasoning can help you make this decision.

As you think ahead, you realize that you generally incur a variety of costs in your business. These include out-of-pocket expenses like supplies, equipment, craft fair entrance fees, and travel expenses when you attend more distant fairs, as well as the opportunity cost of the time you spend designing and assembling cards and managing your booth at craft fairs. After reading this book you realize that you should concentrate on the costs and benefits *directly* associated with attending this particular fair as you make your decision.

For this particular fair, your direct costs are limited to exhibitor registration fees, the cost of supplies used and the time you spend making the cards and minding your booth at the fair. You know that you spend $1.30 on the supplies – paper, embellishments, ribbon, glue, etc. – you use to make a single card. The cost of these supplies constitutes one portion of the marginal cost of producing inventory for the fair.

As we discussed earlier, your time is also a valuable resource. The time you spend making gift cards is therefore an additional cost that needs to be considered. Let's assume that the opportunity cost of the time you would spend making cards is $15 per hour. If it takes 10 minutes (or 1/6 of an hour) to assemble and package a card, then the opportunity cost of the time spent making one card becomes $1/6^{th}$ of the appropriate hourly rate: $15/6=$2.5

This opportunity cost may differ substantially from the dollar value of your current earnings. The opportunity cost of your time includes adjustments for the way you *feel* about the project. For example, you may well be happier assembling cards in a spare bedroom and earning $15 per hour instead of taking on a part-time job as a book-keeper and earning $25 per hour. It all depends on *you* – your likes, dislikes and personal circumstances.

In earlier examples, we defined *marginal cost* as the cost of producing an extra card. In this case, the marginal cost of selling a card at the local craft fair is $1.30+$2.50=$3.80, i.e., the cost of supplies and the time needed to assemble the card itself.

Your *total* opportunity cost also includes the non-refundable exhibitor fee and the value *to you* of the time you spend at the fair. As usual, the value of your time is measured by what you might earn in another activity -- adjusted for any "non-monetary" aspects of attending the fair. Let us suppose that you enjoy chatting with craft fair customers and that your next best option is to earn $150 at a boring part-time job on the day of the fair. Given your feelings about these two options, you conclude that the opportunity cost of your time at the fair is only $100 -- less than what you could earn in the less interesting part-time job.

Table 7-1: Total Cost, Craft Fair Participation

Cards	Supply Cost	Opp. Cost of Production Time	Exhibitor Fee	Opportunity Cost of Time at Fair	Total Opp. Cost
1	$1.30	$2.50	$50	$100	$153.80
5	$6.50	$12.50	$50	$100	$169.00
10	$13.00	$25.00	$50	$100	$188.00
20	$26.00	$50.00	$50	$100	$226.00
30	$39.00	$75.00	$50	$100	$264.00
40	$52.00	$100.00	$50	$100	$302.00
50	$65.00	$125.00	$50	$100	$340.00
60	$78.00	$150.00	$50	$100	$378.00

Table 7-1 summarizes this cost information for a range of production levels.

KEY POINT TO REMEMBER:

❑   Your total cost of an activity includes your out-of-pocket expenses as well as the value *to you* of the time you spend in the activity.

It is important to remember that some regular business expenses have been left out of Table 7-1. The table reports *only* those costs that are the direct result of your decision to participate in this particular craft fair. The fact that you plan to use existing card designs (rather than create new ones) enables you to ignore the opportunity cost of the time you previously spent on creating the design you use. Since this design cost has already been incurred, it is *not* directly associated with this fair and is therefore not relevant to the question at hand. Similar arguments can also be made about other unrelated costs, including the use of existing equipment and facilities or the time you spend managing other aspects of your business. As we mentioned in previous examples, costs that are not affected by the issue at hand can be ignored.

Unit Cost Measures: The information in Table 7-1 allows you to compute the cost of a card sold at the craft fair. Your initial instinct is to divide your total opportunity cost by the number of cards produced − in other words, to compute the *average* opportunity cost of the cards you make. However, after working through the examples found in this book, you realize that you also need to consider the *marginal* cost of your product as you choose your business strategy.   Table 7-2 illustrates the difference between these two cost measures.

Table 7-2: Unit Cost of Craft Fair Participation

Cards	Total Opportunity Cost	Average Opportunity Cost	Marginal Opportunity Cost
1	$153.80	$153.80	
5	$169.00	$33.80	$3.80
10	$188.00	$18.80	$3.80
20	$226.00	$11.30	$3.80
30	$264.00	$8.80	$3.80
40	$302.00	$7.55	$3.80
50	$340.00	$6.80	$3.80
60	$378.00	$6.30	$3.80

As the table illustrates, marginal cost is below average cost in this example: the cost of producing "just one more" – your marginal cost – includes only the value of your production time and materials.   In contrast, your average cost also includes allowances for fixed costs – like your registration fee and the time you spend in your booth at the fair.

In the following sections we will see how to use *both* of these cost measures – as well as market research – to make business decisions.   In general, you need *marginal* cost information to choose your best pricing strategy and *average* cost to determine how much you earned overall.

Consumer Demand

You know that you can never be sure of exactly how many customers will show up at a given event – stormy weather may encourage people to stay home, spectacular weather may lure them outdoors. The best you can do is to rely on your *best guess* about the number of people who will attend the fair and be interested in what you have to sell.

As you plan for a craft fair, your "best guess" should take the form of an estimated number of sales at several different prices. In general, you expect to sell more cards when you lower your asking price. The specific number of anticipated sales will depend on your market research – visits to similar fairs in the recent past, trade forecasts in trade publications, etc. For the purpose of this example, let's assume that Table 7-3 below summarizes your sense of the market – based on the information *available when you have to decide whether or not to register for a particular show.* In other words, you have to rely on your *expectations* about the future since you cannot know what conditions will actually prevail on the day of the show.

Table 7-3: Expected Demand for Gift Cards

Price per Card	Expected Quantity Sold	Expected Total Revenue from Card Sales	Expected Marginal Revenue
$14	22	$308	
$13	26	$338	$7.50
$12	30	$360	$5.50
$11	34	$374	$3.50
$10	38	$380	$1.50
$9	42	$378	-$0.50
$8	46	$368	-$2.50
$7	50	$350	-$4.50
$6	54	$324	-$6.50
$5	58	$290	-$8.50

The table indicates that you are likely to sell *more* cards at *lower* prices. For example, if you set a price of $13 per card, you expect to sell 26 cards at the fair.

KEY POINTS TO REMEMBER:

❑ You generally expect to sell more of your product or service as you lower your asking price.

❑ Just how much more you will sell depends on consumer sensitivity to price changes.

Expected Total and Marginal Sales Revenue: Once you have decided just how sensitive you think customers are to price changes, you can compute your expected total revenue by multiplying your price per card by the number of the cards you expect to sell. For example, if you expect to sell 26 cards at a price of $13 each, then you would anticipate $13x26=$338 in revenue at this price. The third column of Table 7-3 provides the results of this analysis for the relevant range of prices.

Once you have computed your anticipated revenue for the each of the prices under consideration, you can compute your expected *marginal* revenue per card. More precisely, your marginal revenue per card is your *change* in sales revenue divided by the *change* in the number of cards you expect to sell.

Table 7-3 indicates that if you lower your price from $13 to $12, you expect to sell 26-22=4 more cards and will receive $338-308=$30 more in revenue. As a result, your expected marginal revenue at your initial price level is $30/4=$7.5. Similar calculations will allow you to compute the marginal revenue at other price levels. The last column in Table 7-3 provides the results of these calculations.

KEY POINTS TO REMEMBER:

❑   To compute your expected sales revenue at a given
    price level, multiply the price by the number of items
    you expect to sell.

❑   To compute your marginal revenue from additional
    sales, divide the change in your revenue by the change
    in the number of units you sell.

The market information in Table 7-3 illustrates the logical
link between total and marginal sales revenue. You see that your
sales revenue is at its maximum when you set a price of $10. At
this price, your marginal revenue is $1.50 – positive, but as close
to zero as possible in this example. In other words, your last unit
sold netted your business a total of $1.50 in revenue. In general,
you can maximize your revenue by choosing the price that
corresponds to your smallest marginal revenue.

It is important to note that your sales revenue does not
always increase when you lower your asking price. If you lower
your asking price from $10 to $9, your sales revenue actually
falls. Although it may seem odd at first, this result is readily
explained. When you lower your price, you face a trade-off. In
this particular case, your gain from selling 42-38=4 additional
cards is offset by the loss from charging $1 less on the 38 cards
you could have sold at the higher price. As a result, your
marginal revenue is negative; you would earn *more* revenue if
you raised your price.

KEY POINTS TO REMEMBER:

❑ Total sales revenue is at a maximum when marginal revenue is positive, but as small as possible.

❑ If marginal revenue is negative, you can *increase* your sales revenue by *raising* your asking price.

Your Initial Pricing Strategy: The marginal analysis discussed in previous examples can now help you identify the best business strategy for this craft business. The general rule developed earlier was to expand your business until the benefit to you of further expansion no longer covered the cost to you of the activity. The principle operates on two levels in the current example: both in your decision of whether or not to register for the up-coming craft fair and in your choice of pricing strategy if you do actually attend. In practice, it is useful to answer these questions in "reverse order": first to decide how much you could benefit if you did attend the fair and only then to decide whether or not it makes sense to register.

Table 7-4 combines the information found in Table 7-2 and Table 7-3 above and can be used to help you

• choose the most appropriate asking price for your cards (given the available information); and

• determine the corresponding amount of inventory you would need to bring to the fair.

In particular, this table shows your expected earnings in excess of opportunity cost for the range of product prices you are considering.

Table 7-4: Expected Earnings from Gift Cards

Price per Card	Expected Quantity Sold	Expected Total Revenue	Expected Marginal Revenue	Total Opp. Cost	Marg. Opp. Cost	Expected Earnings
$14	22	$308		$233.60	$3.80	$74.40
$13	26	$338	$7.50	$248.80	$3.80	$89.20
$12	*30*	*$360*	*$5.50*	*$264.00*	*$3.80*	*$96.00*
$11	34	$374	$3.50	$279.20	$3.80	$94.80
$10	38	$380	$1.50	$294.40	$3.80	$85.60
$9	42	$378	-$0.50	$309.60	$3.80	$68.40
$8	46	$368	-$2.50	$324.80	$3.80	$43.20
$7	50	$350	-$4.50	$340.00	$3.80	$10.00
$6	54	$324	-$6.50	$355.20	$3.80	-$31.20
$5	58	$290	-$8.50	$370.40	$3.80	-$80.40

Table 7-4 shows that, given your current market and cost information, your greatest earnings occur when you charge $12 per card. This result confirms our earlier observations about marginal revenue and marginal cost: your greatest earnings occur at the point where the additional revenue received from selling an extra card ($5.50) is just above the marginal cost of producing that card ($3.80).

At a price of $12, you expect to sell 30 cards at the fair and generate $360 in sales revenue. You will also incur two types of cost if you go ahead with this project: out-of-pocket expenses and the opportunity cost of your time. As Table 7-1 indicates, you will need to spend $39 for supplies and $50 for your exhibitor's fee. The value of the time you spend making the 30 cards for this fair is $75; the value of the time you spend minding your booth at the fair is $100. As a result, your total opportunity cost is $264, and you expect to earn $246 in excess of these opportunity costs.

In general, you can identify such your "optimal pricing strategy" in a variety of ways. For example, you could compute your expected earnings at each price level, or your could simply compare the revenue and opportunity cost implications of lowering your price and choose the lowest price at which you can cover the marginal cost of selling an extra card. Although both techniques lead to the same answer, the latter is likely to be simpler in practice.

KEY POINT TO REMEMBER:

❑   Your expected earnings are highest when your expected marginal revenue just covers you marginal opportunity cost.

Earnings from Your Business Venture: It is important to remember that you play two roles in this example: that of employee and that of entrepreneur.   Each of these roles represents a distinct source of business earnings. By thinking of yourself as a worker and (conceptually) paying yourself a wage, you are treating your own time as a real cost and are explicitly taking into account the earnings foregone by passing up a different job option. As an entrepreneur, you get to keep any money left over after you have paid your bills and compensated yourself for the opportunity cost of your time. As a result, your total   expected   benefit   from   entering   the   craft   fair   is $75+$100+$96=$271: the value of your time *plus* your earnings in excess of your opportunity cost.

KEY POINT TO REMEMBER:

❑   Your total earnings from a business include both the sales revenue set aside to cover the opportunity cost of your time, as well as any revenue received in excess of your total opportunity cost.

Adapting to New Information:

At this point, you have reason to believe that it would be to your advantage to enter the craft fair. You expect to sell enough to cover *all* of your costs (including compensating yourself for earnings foregone in another activity) and have $96 left over. On the basis of your research, you decide to send in your non-refundable $50 application fee.

Unfortunately, you don't always get what you expect. You may, for example, discover on the day of the craft fair that unseasonable weather will severely reduce attendance – and the number of sales that you will be able to make. Marginal analysis and opportunity cost reasoning can help you figure out how to adjust to new information. For the example developed in this section, we will that you have reason to go ahead with your initial plans even though you are no longer able to cover the full cost of attending the fair.

On the day of the fair, you will generally have a different set of options than you did when you initially decided to register for the fair. In other words, some of your choices will already have been made. If these decisions cannot be undone, they are best taken as given – issues already settled as you consider whether or not to go ahead with your plans to attend.

For example, by the day of the fair, you will already have sent in your check covering the non-refundable exhibitor's fee. Since nothing you do now will change this expense, it is no longer relevant to your decision. This cost is *sunk* – you cannot get a refund if you do not show up at your booth. As a result, it may make sense to attend the fair even if you cannot earn enough to cover the cost of your entrance fee. We will see below that if you can cover at least *part* of the fee, you will be better off participating in the fair than staying at home.

By the day of the fair you will also have spent time making the cards you plan to sell. Obviously, you cannot recover this time and use it to do something else. As a result, the opportunity cost of the cards in inventory – for the purpose of your current decisions – is no longer the cost of the time and materials needed to make them. Instead, the opportunity cost of your inventory is now whatever you could get for your cards in a different market – for example by selling them to a local retailer or at a later craft fair. In the following sections, we will see how this distinction affects your decisions on the day of the fair.

New Consumer Demand: Let us suppose that Table 7-5 reflects the new market information you learn on the day of the craft fair.

Table 7-5: Consumer Demand Revised to Reflect New Information

Price per Card	Expected Quantity Sold	Expected Total Revenue	Expected Marginal Revenue
$14	8	$112	
$13	11	$143	$10.33
$12	14	$168	$8.33
$11	17	$187	$6.33
$10	20	$200	$4.33
$9	23	$207	$2.33
$8	26	$208	$0.33
$7	29	$203	-$1.67
$6	30*	$180	-$23

*Indicates that you could expect to sell at least 30 cards (the total number you have in inventory) on the day of the fair.

Given the weather conditions on the day of the fair, you now realize that you are likely to sell only 14 cards at your original asking price of $12. As Table 7-5 shows, you now expect to earn your highest revenue at a price of $8 per card. Furthermore, you expect to sell all 30 of your cards only if you lower your asking price to $6.

You now face a modified version of your original business decision: whether or not to go ahead with your plan to participate in the fair and whether or not to reduce your asking price (if you do in fact attend). These questions are best answered by looking at updated versions of both your marginal revenue and your marginal opportunity cost. As we will see, it makes to sense to attend the fair and lower your price in this scenario.

The last column of Table 7-5 provides information concerning your new expected marginal revenue. As before, to compute your marginal revenue you divide the change in your sales revenue by the change in the number of cards sold. For example, if you lower your price from $12 to $11, you expect to sell 3 more cards and receive $19 more in revenue. Your new expected marginal revenue is therefore $19/3=$6.33.

New Opportunity Cost: Your revised opportunity cost is a bit more complicated. The way you adapt to new information on the day of the fair will depend largely upon what else you can do with the cards you have already made. In other words, it your decision will depend on the current opportunity cost of the cards themselves.

Since you cannot reclaim the time and the supplies you used to produce your inventory, these items no longer have an opportunity cost. Specifically, Table 7-1 lists the total cost of 30 cards as $264 – the value of supplies used, the exhibitor fee for the craft fair, and the time spent making the cards and staffing your booth at the fair.   However, only some of these costs are still relevant to your current decisions. On the day of the fair, these production costs are "sunk" – all except for the $100 opportunity cost of the time you would spend at the fair. Nothing you do now can change the fact that you have already incurred $164 to produce your inventory. As a result, it is best to ignore this $164 cost as you make decisions on the day of the fair.

Nevertheless, the cards themselves now have an opportunity cost. In principle, you could sell them at a later craft fair (and incur a new exhibitor fee), sell them wholesale to a local gift shop, or use them yourself. For the purposes of this example, let us suppose that your best alternative use for unsold cards is to sell them to a local gift shop for $2 each. In other words, each card has an opportunity cost of $2.

The value to you of time you would have to spend in your booth at the fair represents the other component of your current opportunity cost. For this example we assume as before that the value to you of the time you would spend at the fair itself is $100.

Table 7-6 shows how to combine these assumptions to determine the updated opportunity cost of your inventory.

Table 7-6: Opportunity Cost, the Day of the Fair

Expected Quantity Sold at Fair	Sunk Cost of Inventory (30 cards)	Updated Opp. Cost of Cards Sold	Updated Opp. Cost of Time at the Fair	Updated Total Opp. Cost of Craft Fair Sales	Marginal Opp. Cost
8	$164	$16	$100	$116	$2
11	$164	$22	$100	$122	$2
14	$164	$28	$100	$128	$2
17	$164	$34	$100	$134	$2
20	$164	$40	$100	$140	$2
23	$164	$46	$100	$146	$2
26	$164	$52	$100	$152	$2
29	$164	$58	$100	$158	$2
30	$164	$64	$100	$164	$2

Table 7-7 combines your information about customer demand from Table 7-5 and the opportunity cost of your inventory on the day of the fair. Using the marginal cost approach developed in previous sections, we see that your best alternative is to go to the fair, reduce your price from $12 to $9 per card, plan to sell 23 cards at the fair, and sell the remaining cards to the local gift store. At this price, the marginal revenue from selling all cards – both at the fair and to the gift store owner – just covers the opportunity cost of the items sold.

Table 7-7: Revised Expected Earnings from the Craft Fair

Price per Card	Expected Quantity Sold	Expected Craft Fair Revenue	Expected Marginal Revenue	Opp. Cost of Craft Fair Sales	Marg. Opp. Cost	Rev. less Opp. Cost
Craft Fair Sales:						
$14	8	$112		$116	$2	-$4
$13	11	$143	$10.33	$122	$2	$21
$12	14	$168	$8.33	$128	$2	$40
$11	17	$187	$6.33	$134	$2	$53
$10	20	$200	$4.33	$140	$2	$60
$9	*23*	*$207*	*$2.33*	*$146*	*$2*	*$61*
$8	26	$208	$0.33	$152	$2	$56
$7	29	$203	-$1.67	$158	$2	$45
$6	30	$180	-$23	$160	$2	$20
Gift Store Sales (used to define opportunity cost):						
$2	30	$60	-$120	$60	$2	$0

Table 7-7 also shows why other options are worse. If you left your price at $12, you would only expect to sell 14 cards at the fair. At this price, you understand that the added revenue from lowering your price would cover more than the opportunity cost of your inventory. As a result, it would be profitable do so. You also know that you would maximize your sales revenue at a price of $8 per card. However, at this price the marginal revenue from the last few cards sold ($.33 per card) was below the marginal cost per card ($2). As a result, you realize that it would be profitable to *raise* your price. If you chose not to attend the fair at all – and sold all of your inventory to the local gift store – you would only cover your marginal opportunity cost of $2 per card.

Table 7-8 confirms the insight that attending the fair and charging $9 per card is your best strategy. Although you do not cover all your production costs at this price, you do minimize your losses. Since you have already paid your entrance fee for the craft fair and have spent the time and money needed to create 30 cards, the best you can do is limit your loss to $43.

Table 7-8: Net Returns from Craft Fair Participation

Price	Quantity	Craft Fair Sales	Gift Store Sales	Total Revenue	Total Production Cost	Revenue Less Cost
Attend the Craft Fair (and sell remaining cards to gift store):						
$14	8	$112	$44	$156	$264	-$108
$13	11	$143	$38	$181	$264	-$83
$12	14	$168	$32	$200	$264	-$64
$11	17	$187	$26	$213	$264	-$51
$10	20	$200	$20	$220	$264	-$44
$9	23	$207	$14	$221	$264	-$43
$8	26	$208	$8	$216	$264	-$48
$7	29	$203	$2	$205	$264	-$59
$6	30	$180	$0	$180	$264	-$84
Sell All Cards to Gift Store:						
$2	30	0	$60	$60	$164	-$100

Other circumstances are likely to lead to other outcomes. If craft fair attendance had been *better* than initially expected, the above logic would lead you to consider *raising* your asking price. If the opportunity cost of your time at the fair had been higher, then it might have been worthwhile to stay home after all and sell your inventory to the local gift store

In any case, it is essential to ask at each point in time what questions remain unanswered, what issues are unresolved – and devote yourself to finding the best available solutions. The sunk cost of decisions already made is best ignored.

ॐ ॐ ॐ

OFFERING A DISCOUNT TO SPECIAL CUSTOMERS OR CLIENTS

In some situations, it may also be possible to improve your bottom line by offering a discount to special groups of people –

even if it means charging them a price that appears to be "below cost". This unusual result becomes less surprising when we remember that cost can be measured in different ways, and that the cost of producing "just one more" may be radically different than the average cost of providing your good or service to all of your customers.

Consider, for example, the issue raised by one of the members of the Planning Committee of the (hypothetical) Association of Professional Professionals. The Association holds an annual convention in different cities around the world. The Planning Committee expects 400 members to attend this year. With this many people in attendance, the Planning Committee knows that the Association will have to pay the conference hotel $90 per registrant for a package deal that covers the cost of conference rooms and catered coffee breaks.

The Planning Committee is trying to decide whether or not to offer a student discount. In the past, the Association has charged its members a uniform fee designed to cover the expected cost of the conference. For the current year, this policy would mean charging members $90 to register for the conference.

Some Planning Committee members have argued that offering a student discount could meet two objectives at the same time: this policy change could attract potential new members *and* improve the current finances of the organization. The specific argument for this proposal works as follows. If students are offered a 50 percent discount (i.e., charged a registration fee of $45), then 40 graduate students are likely to attend. As a result of this increased attendance, the conference hotel is willing to charge a lower fee per participant. Specifically, if conference attendance rises to 440, the Association will have to pay the hotel only $85 per participant. Table 7-9 summarizes the implications of these options for total conference costs.

Table 7-9: Average and Marginal Cost of Holding a Conference

Attendees	Hotel Cost per Participant (Average Cost)	Total Cost	Marginal Cost per Participant
400	$90	$36,000	
440	$85	$37,400	$35

Although it seems unlikely, a 50 percent student discount can actually work to the benefit of the Association even though it means a charging a price *below* the average cost per participant. Marginal cost analysis can help show why. As Table 7-9 indicates, the total bill for the conference rises by only $1,400 when 40 students attend. In other words, the marginal cost for these participants is only $1,400/50 or $35. If the Association offers students a reduced fee of $45, it will earn more than enough to cover the marginal cost of their participation.

Table 7-10: Conference Revenues

	No Student Discount		Discount Offered	
Regular Members:	400		400	
Registration Fee:	$90		$90	
Registration Revenue, Regular Members		$36,000		$36,000
Student Attendees:	-		40	
Registration Fee:	-		$45	
Registration Revenue, Students:		-		$1,800
Total Revenue from Attendees		$36,000		$37,800
Total Participants	400		440	
Hotel Charge per Participant	$90		$85	
Total Hotel Charge		$36,000		$37,400
Revenue *less* Charges		$0		$400

Table 7-10 provides a side-by-side comparison of these two

scenarios. When no discount is offered, registration revenues exactly cover the hotel bill for the conference. However, when a student discount is offered, the Association actually earns $400 over and above the amount needed to cover the hotel bill for the larger conference. Since the Association qualifies for a "quantity discount" from the hotel when it sponsors a larger conference, the Association can offer a student discount and enhance its bottom line – even though the discounted fee is below its average cost per participant.

This situation occurs more often than you might think. The publishers of academic, professional and trade publications routinely set different prices for students, libraries and independent professionals. For example, the *Rand Journal of Economics* charges $60 per year for an individual subscription, offers students a discounted rate of $25 per year, and requires "institutions" to pay $170 per year. Such pricing strategies have the general effect of charging higher prices to customers with a higher "willingness-to-pay."

A variety of retailers have started to use a related means of charging different prices to different customers: the "frequent buyer's club." National chains of grocery stores, book sellers, and pharmacies, as well as local shops selling quilt fabrics, art stamps or other craft supplies, now routinely offer discounts upon presentation of a membership card. In some stores, customers must pay a fee to join the club; in other cases, it is only necessary to remember to carry the membership card. In any case, the purpose remains the same: the retailers offer selective discounts in order to increase sales. Such strategies can work well as long as it is possible to keep the relevant customer groups separate – i.e., as long as customers do not band together and share membership privileges among themselves (without individually meeting the requirements that membership entails).

❧ ❧ ❧

ACCOUNTING FOR COMMON COSTS

The accounting profession faces a difficult challenge: it must design a standardized set of accounts that will tell corporate managers both how much it cost to get the *last* unit of product out the door and how much money the *entire* company made in any given period of time. This dual task is complicated by the fact that most companies have some costs that are *fixed* (i.e., invariant with the level of output) and other costs that are *variable* (i.e., change as the level of production changes). The problem of designing a system of accounts becomes even more complex when the company has more than one line of business – distinct lines of business typically share corporate resources (and naturally the fixed cost associated with common resources).

Accountants have developed a variety of conventions for assigning fixed costs to different lines of business. Shared costs are often allocated on the basis of output, sales volume, labor cost, square feet of floor space occupied, etc. These rules enable analysts to define the profit for the company *as a whole*. Unfortunately, they may produce misleading results when comparing the profitability of different divisions within the company.

Consider the case of Why Knot, Inc., a (hypothetical) retail store selling ties, scarves and umbrellas. The following table indicates the prices charged, the quantities sold in a typical month, and the wholesale prices paid by the shop.

Table 7-11: Why Knot, Inc.: Prices, Costs, and Sales Volume

	Scarves	Ties	Umbrellas
Unit Price	80	40	20
Quantity Sold	300	500	800
Unit Wholesale Cost	40	32	15

Since these three types of merchandise are sold in the same shop, the general cost of running the shop – rent, utilities, salaries for sales staff, etc. – represent a shared cost for these three lines of business. The next table indicates the contribution made to shared costs by each type of merchandise.

Table 7-12: Why Knot, Inc.: Contributions to Shared Costs

	Scarves	Ties	Umbrellas
Revenue	24,000	20,000	16,000
Cost of Merchandise	12,000	16,000	12,000
Contribution to Common Costs and Profit	12,000	4,000	4,000

Clearly all three lines of business are making a positive contribution to the company's "bottom line."

If common costs are truly fixed (i.e., independent of the variety of merchandise sold), then Why Knot, Inc. has higher profits when selling all three products than it would have with only one or two types of merchandise. However, this point may be obscured when the cost of running the shop is allocated by a pre-specified accounting rule.

Equal Split of Shared Costs: Suppose that it costs $18,000 a month to run the store and that this cost does not depend on the number of or variety of items sold. Consider first the simplest rule for allocating overhead cost: each line of business must contribute the *same* amount before it is considered profitable. The table below indicates the profit implied by this rule for each type of merchandise. Note: parentheses (.) indicate a negative number – a loss.

Table 7-13: Equal Split of Shared Costs

	Scarves	Ties	Umbrellas
Revenue	24,000	20,000	16,000
Cost of Merchandise	12,000	16,000	12,000
Common Cost Share	6,000	6,000	6,000
Profit (with equal split for common costs):	6,000	(2,000)	(2,000)

This rule makes it seem as though the store is making a loss on *both* ties and umbrellas, something quite far from the truth. (Check your intuition: how would you argue that the two product lines were in fact profitable?)

Allocating Shared Costs on the Basis of Variable Costs: Consider next another common accounting practice: allocate common costs on the basis of the "cost of goods sold" (listed above as "Cost of Merchandise:). The table below provides the implied profits by type of merchandise.

Table 7-14: Allocating Shared Costs by Cost of Goods Sold

	Scarves	Ties	Umbrellas
Revenue	24,000	20,000	16,000
Cost of Merchandise	12,000	16,000	12,000
Common Cost Share (based on cost of Merchandise)	5,400	7,200	5,400
Profit:	6,600	(3,200)	(1400)

Once again, two lines of business appear to be generating a loss, even though the store is *more profitable* with these all three types of merchandise than it would be with either one or two product lines. Similar problems arise if we try to allocate shared costs on the basis of sales revenue.

Allocating Shared Costs on the Basis of Profitability: What accounting method avoids this confusion? At a minimum we need to be certain that each line of business covers its "direct" costs, including the cost of any "common" resources that could be avoided if the firm had fewer distinct lines of business. If all common costs are truly fixed, then they can be allocated in a way that assesses each product line an equal proportion of its *potential* contribution to shared costs. The following table works out the implications of this approach.

Table 7-15: Allocating Shared Costs by Ability to Pay

	Scarves	Ties	Umbrellas
Revenue	24,000	20,000	16,000
Cost of Merchandise	12,000	16,000	12,000
Common Cost Share (based on division contributions)	10,800	3,600	3,600
Profit:	1,200	400	400

In this example, the total amount of money available to cover shared expenditures is $20,000. Once this amount is known, each line of merchandise could be assigned an amount proportional to its contribution to the total. Under this rule, the scarves product line would be assigned 60 percent of the common cost (i.e., 60 percent of 18,000) since this product line contributed 60 percent of the funds available to pay for common costs and profit; "ties" and "umbrellas" would each be assigned 20 percent of the overhead cost. Under this rule, *all* product lines show an operating profit, since all divisions made a positive contribution to shared costs.

This rule has the virtue of being equitable on a percentage basis. In the Why Knot, Inc. example, each line of business essentially faces the same 90 percent "tax" rate. Since 90 percent of the available $20,000 was needed to pay for shared costs, each product line ends up contributing 90 percent of its available funds to the common cause (and reporting the remaining 10 percent as profit).

Unfortunately, no rule is perfect, including this one. Since managers are essentially taxed on the basis of their reported divisional operating surpluses, they may have less incentive to maximize the surpluses reported by their respective divisions. This approach also has the effect of reducing the effectiveness of some compensation schemes. If bonuses are based on divisional profit *after* a tax for shared costs has been levied, managers will realize that the marginal benefit (to themselves and/or to their divisions) of additional effort is reduced by the amount of the overhead assessment.

ꙮ ꙮ ꙮ

LESSONS LEARNED

By now you should begin to see the importance of asking the *right* question -- of identifying the relevant opportunity costs and using marginal analysis to find the answer that works best for you. For example, looking at the wrong cost measure could lead you to set a price that is too high or abandon a profitable line of business.

As you grow more familiar with the approach developed in this book, you will see how it can be applied to far more situations than those mentioned here. With practice, you can use it to figure out

- whether or not you should accept credit cards; (does the convenience to your customers bring in enough new business to offset the fees you must pay to the banks issuing the cards?);

and

- when you should lease rather than buy equipment (does the opportunity cost of the funds you would use for the purchase exceed the value to you of the lease payments?);

or even

- why leases that require you to pay a percentage of your revenues will give you the incentive to lower your price (the fee lowers your marginal revenue and gives you the incentive to choose a level of business with a lower marginal cost);

and

- why you should set your price to earn as much revenue as possible if you are stuck with inventory that has no alternative uses (if an item has no opportunity cost, then it has a marginal cost of zero and should be sold at a price that implies a marginal revenue of zero).

The choice of questions depends on you!

≋ ≋ ≋

8

Where Do We
Go from Here?

By this point you will have seen two basic business principles – opportunity cost and marginal analysis – used to make a variety of common business decisions. I hope you will have started to think of these principles as the basis for a practical approach to problem-solving, one that helps you choose among the available alternatives by encouraging you to focus on the impact of your current decisions.

It is now up to you to adapt this approach to suit *your* needs. The remainder of this chapter gives you a range of places to look for more information.

≋ ≋ ≋

ON-LINE RESOURCES

As you probably already know, the Web represents a rich opportunity for gathering information, getting advice and – for some – gaining new business. Table 8-1 lists several Web sites that currently provide information of particular interest to small business owners. About.com provides "how-to" advice on almost anything; the link listed below will take you to their section on running various types of craft businesses. *The Crafts Report* is a monthly trade magazine aimed at both craft retailers and manufacturers. The Small Business Administration site is maintained by the Federal agency established to assist small-scale entrepreneurs. Although both Quicken and Staples obviously hope to use their web sites to sell products and services, you can also find a great deal of useful financial information on these two sites.

Table 8-1: Small Business References

About.com, Arts and Crafts Business:	artsandcrafts.about.com/mbody.htm	The business section of a great "how-to" web site.
The Crafts Report	www.craftsreport.com	A monthly trade publication for people in the craft business.
Small Business Administration	www.sba.gov	Uncle Sam's site for small businesses.
Quicken On-Line	www.quicken.com/small_business	The advice section of a useful financial web site.
Staples On-Line, Run Your Business	www.staples.com/BizServices	The advice and services section from this office supply chain.

Table 8-2 provides a list of links to Federal government sites of interest to a broad range of business owners. Through the Bureau of the Public Debt you can set up a low-cost account that enables you to buy U.S. Treasury securities directly from the government and thereby avoid paying the fees generally charged by brokers. The IRS web site gives you access to downloadable versions of virtually all Federal tax forms, instruction booklets, and other publications. Lastly, FedBizOps is a site that maintains a searchable listing of Federal government procurement opportunities. Many of these "Requests for Proposals" are earmarked for small businesses, so it may be worth looking to see if you are offering services that Uncle Sam may wish to buy.

Table 8-2: Federal Government Web Sites

Bureau of the Public Debt	www.publicdebt.treas.gov	Buy Treasury securities direct from Uncle Sam: no brokerage fees.
IRS: The Digital Daily	www.irs.ustreas.gov	Get advice on Federal tax issues.
FedBizOps	www.fbodaily.com	Get info on contracting with the Federal Government.

Table 8-3 lists a number of my favorite places to start looking for all sorts of information. CEO Express provides a well-chosen set of links to help you find everything from today's weather report and stock market performance to customized roadmaps and the best deals on new computer equipment. Resources for Economists on the Internet is a multi-level Web site devoted to economic and financial information. Each link in Bill Goffe's directory is annotated to help you find the data you need as quickly as possible. The remaining sites provide slightly different searching opportunities, so it will often be worth your while to consult more than one of them if you do not find the answer to your question on the first try.

Table 8-3:   General e-References

CEO Express	www.ceoexpress.com	A one-page collection of very useful links.
Resources for Economists on the Internet	rfe.wustl.edu	Bill Goffe's annotated collection of economic and financial info.
Yahoo	www.yahoo.com	The pioneering search engine.
Hotbot/Lycos	www.hotbot.lycos.com and search.lycos.com	My favorite places to start looking.
Google	google.com	Another great place to search.
Dogpile	www.dogpile.com	Submit a query to multiple search engines.
Ask Jeeves	www.askjeeves.com	Ask questions in plain English!

≈ ≈ ≈

BOOKS OF INTEREST:

The following is a list of recent books that provide advice on the nitty-gritty details of setting up and running your own business.

Brabec, Barbara. *Handmade for Profit*. New York: M. Evans, 1996.

Folger, Liz. *The Stay-at-Home Mom's Guide to Making Money from Home*. Roseville, CA: Prima Publishing, 2000.

Huff, Priscilla Y. *101 Best Home-Based Businesses for Women*, Roseville, CA: Prima Publishing, 1998.

Restuccia, Nancy. *Publish Your Patterns! How to Write, Print and Market Your Designs*. Make It Easy Sewing & Crafts Publishing, 2002.

Rosen, Wendy. *Crafting as a Business*. Baltimore: Rosen Group, 1998.

Simon, Julian L. *How to Start and Operate a Mail-Order Business*, 5th Ed. New York: McGraw-Hill, 1993.

Wittig Albert, Susan. *Work of Her Own: A Woman's Guide to Success off the Career Track*. New York: Putnam. 1994.

〰 〰 〰

Glossary

Average Cost

Your total cost divided by your total production volume. Also known as unit cost.

Business Earnings

The difference between your revenue and the direct cost of *all* resources used in production (including the opportunity cost of your time). Maximizing business earnings is generally assumed to be the goal of entrepreneurs.

Incremental Cost

The additional cost incurred when you expand production by a small amount. See also *marginal cost*.

Incremental Revenue

The additional revenue earned when you increase your sales volume by a small amount. See also *marginal revenue*.

Marginal Cost

In general, the cost of producing *one* extra unit of a product or service. To compute your current marginal cost, figure out how much your total cost will increase after a small change in your production volume and then divide this cost increase by the number of additional units produced. For example, if you must spend \$1200 more to produce 8 extra units then your marginal cost is \$1200/8 = \$150.

Marginal   The added revenue earned by selling
Revenue   one extra unit of a product or service.
                    To compute your current marginal
                    revenue, figure out how much revenue
                    you would earn if you sold a few extra
                    units. (Be certain to include the impact
                    of any price changes on current sales.)
                    Divide the change in revenue by the
                    change in the number of units sold.

Profit   Generally, the difference between total
                    revenue and total cost. However, the
                    relevant measure of profit depends on
                    the specific question of interest. The
                    IRS definition of taxable income is
                    typically different from the measure of
                    business earnings used to evaluate new
                    business opportunities: the cost
                    measure used to compute taxable
                    income will generally include direct
                    costs (i.e., those directly associated with
                    a particular business venture), sunk
                    costs and costs shared among several
                    activities.

Opportunity   The value to you of whatever you
Cost   forego when you make a particular
                    choice. Examples include wages not
                    earned when you go into business for
                    yourself, time not spent with family and
                    friends when you go to work, and
                    dividends or interest not earned when
                    you invest your personal saving in your
                    own business.

Sunk Cost   Expenditures that were irrevocably
                    incurred in the past. Since by

assumption they cannot be changed, they are not relevant to current and future decisions: you will be stuck with these costs no matter what you decide to do. Examples include non-refundable payments actually made in the past or simply promised in the past for a future date.

Taxable Business Income

The difference between your business revenue and the business expenses recognized by the IRS. Note that this measure of your income will include both the opportunity cost of your time and your business earnings.

Total Employee Compensation

The sum of all earnings from your activities as an employee. Includes the value to you of employer-provided benefits as well as your salary, wage and any overtime payments.

Index

21t; expected per hour worked for part-time workers, 22, 22t; in
Federal civil service, 19, 20t; key points to remember, 23
Emergency Medical Technicians (EMTs) (case example), 7, 16–17,
26–27nn3–4; expected earnings, 16–17; expected earnings per
hour worked, 22, 22t; opportunity cost summary, 53, 53t; shift
deferentials, 16
employee compensation. *see* compensation
employees: distinctions between contractors and, 74–76; job attributes
of, 75. *see also* salaried professionals or employees; workers
EMTs. *see* Emergency Medical Technicians
equal job satisfaction, 34–37
equal split of shared costs, 136–137
equipment: leasing *versus* buying, 139
expansion, 65–94; benefits of, 80–83; considerations for, 65; costs of,
73–80; ideal strategy for, 83; key points to remember, 72;
service business opportunities, 84–86
expected marginal revenues, 115
expected marginal sales revenue, 121–122
expenses: associated with new business ventures, 48, 48t; fixed, 97; key
points to remember, 49; total, 98; travel, 97. *see also* cost(s)

F
fabrics, custom-designed (case example), 89–90; average cost of fabric,
89, 89t; marginal cost of fabric, 90, 90t
FedBizOps, 143, 143t
Federal civil service: hourly earnings in, 19, 20t; total compensation in,
19, 19t
Federal government web sites, 142–143, 143t
FICA taxes, 27nn8–9
fixed costs, 105–106, 135; key points to remember, 107
fixed expenditures, 97
fixed prices, selling at, 80–83
framed antique tiles (case example), 63
Fran (Registered Nurse). *see* Registered Nurses
frequent buyer's clubs, 134
full-time hourly workers: example, 11–15; key points to remember, 15;
opportunity cost for, 11–12, 12t; total compensation for, 11–15

G
gains, taxable, 59–60

gift cards (case example): expected demand for, 120, 120*t*; expected
    earnings from, 123, 124*t*, 125
Goffe, Bill, 143
goods and services mix, 114
goods sold, cost of, 55; allocating shared costs by, 137, 137*t*
graphic artists (case example), 89–90
greeting cards (case example): supply costs, 67, 67*t*
growth, 65–94; considerations for, 65; key points to remember, 72

H
health benefits, 10
home office deduction, 60, 64n2
Hotbot/Lycos, 144*t*
hourly billing rates, target, 40, 40*t*
hourly compensation, 29; contractor hours to replace current
    compensation, 31, 31*t*; minimum desired rates, 35–36, 35*t*;
    overtime pay, 38; target billing rates, 40, 40*t*
hourly earnings: computing, 18–23; example, 50–51, 51*t*; expected for
    hourly employees, 21, 22*t*; expected for salaried employees, 20,
    21*t*; expected per hour worked for part-time workers, 22, 22*t*; in
    Federal civil service, 19, 20*t*; key points to remember, 23
hourly rates: fewer hours, higher reservation billing rate option, 36–37;
    longer hours, higher reservation billing rate option, 36;
    minimum desired, 35–36, 35*t*; for part-time workers, 16, 16*t*;
    same schedule, lower reservation billing rate option, 36
hourly workers: contractors, 29–41; expected earnings per hour, 21,
    22*t*; fewer hours, higher reservation billing rate option, 36–37;
    key points to remember, 18; longer hours, higher reservation
    billing rate option, 36; minimum number of hours needed, 33;
    part-time earnings for, 38, 39*t*; same schedule, lower reservation
    billing rate option, 36; total compensation for, 23–24, 25*t*–26*t*
hourly workers, full-time: example, 11–15; key points to remember, 15;
    opportunity cost for, 11–12, 12*t*; total compensation for, 11–15
hourly workers, part-time: example, 16–17; expected earnings per hour
    worked, 22, 22*t*; hourly wage rates for, 16, 16*t*; opportunity cost
    for, 16–17, 17*t*; total compensation for, 16–17

I
income, taxable: definition of, 149; key points to remember, 60; from
    new ventures, 59–60
incremental costs, 48, 66–68; definition of, 147. *see also* marginal costs

R

Rand Journal of Economics, 134

rates, billing: fewer hours, higher reservation billing rate option, 36–37; longer hours, higher reservation billing rate option, 36; same schedule, lower reservation billing rate option, 36

rates, hourly: fewer hours, higher reservation billing rate option, 36–37; longer hours, higher reservation billing rate option, 36; minimum desired, 35–36, 35*t*; for part-time workers, 16, 16*t*; same schedule, lower reservation billing rate option, 36

Registered Nurses (case example), 7, 11–15; contractor hours to replace current compensation, 31, 31*t*; expected base pay, 13; expected earnings per hour, 21, 22*t*; fewer hours, higher reservation billing rate option, 36–37; finding equal job satisfaction, 34–37; hours paid at base wage, 12–13; insurance benefits, 14; just breaking even, 30–33; longer hours, higher reservation billing rate option, 36; opportunity cost for, 11–12, 12*t*; opportunity cost summary, 53, 53*t*; other benefits, 14–15; overtime pay, 13; as part-time contractor, 37–39; same schedule, lower reservation billing rate option, 36; self-employment taxes, 14

rent and sales commission, 55–56

resources: books of interest, 144–145; on-line, 64n2, 141–144; small business references, 142–143, 142*t*

Resources for Economists on the internet, 143, 144*t*

retail stores (case examples), 87–89, 108–109; average costs, 87, 87*t*; contributions to shared costs, 135–136, 136*t*; equal split of shared costs, 136–137; marginal costs, 88, 88*t*; marginal revenue for, 108–109, 109*t*; prices, costs, and sales volume, 135–136, 135*t*

retail ventures: antiques business example, 54–59; clothing accessories store example, 135–136, 135*t*, 136*t*; clothing store example, 108–109; earnings from, 62, 62*t*; evaluation of, 62; framed antique tiles example, 63; jewelry store example, 87–89; selling products, 43–64

retirement benefits, 9–10

returns, net, 130, 131*t*

revenue(s): conference example, 133–134, 133*t*; craft fair example, 101, 102*t*; weekly, psychology example, 86, 86*t*

revenue, incremental, 68–69; definition of, 147; key ponts to remember, 69

revenue, marginal, 68–69; bakery example, 108, 108*t*; clothing store example, 108–109, 109*t*; definition of, 148, 149; examples, 108–

109, 108*t*, 109*t*; expected, 115, 121–122; key ponts to
remember, 69, 100
revenue, marginal sales, 99–100; expected, 121–122; key points to
remember, 122
revenue, sales: increasing, 123; key points to remember, 122;
maximizing, 103–104, 105
revenue, total sales, 99; expected, 121–122; key points to remember,
123

S
salaried professionals or employees: example, 7–11; expected earnings
per hour, 20, 21*t*; key points to remember, 11; opportunity cost
for, 7–8, 8*t*; total compensation for, 7–11, 23–24, 24*t*
salary, base, 8. *see also* compensation
sales commission, 55–56
sales revenue: increasing, 123; key points to remember, 122;
maximizing, 103–104, 105
sales revenue, marginal, 99–100; expected, 121–122; key points to
remember, 122
sales revenue, total, 99; expected, 121–122; key points to remember,
123
sales volume, example, 135–136, 135*t*
Sally (EMT). *see* Emergency Medical Technicians (EMTs)
scale of operation: choosing, 71–72; desired, 71–72
scale of service businesses, 84–86
self-employment taxes: examples, 9, 14; key points to remember, 11
selling products, 43–64; antiques example, 57–58, 58*t*; earnings from,
57–58, 58*t*; at fixed price, 80–83; framed antique tiles example,
63; more at a lower price, 96–103. *see also* retail ventures
service business: example, 84–86; expansion opportunities in, 84–86;
scale of, 84–86
services, pricing, 95–112
shared costs: allocating by ability to pay, 138, 138*t*; allocating by cost
of goods sold, 137, 137*t*; allocating on basis of profitability,
137–139; allocating on basis of variable costs, 137;
contributions to, 135–136, 136*t*; equal split of, 136–137, 136*t*
shift deferentials, examples, 16, 26–27nn3–4
Small Business Administration, 141–142, 142*t*
small business references, 142–143, 142*t*
special customers or clients: discounts to, 131–134

U.S. Treasury, 142

V
variable costs, 135; allocating shared costs on basis of, 137
ventures: earnings from, 47–48, 47*t*, 125; expenses associated with, 48,
    48*t*; key points to remember, 54, 59; maintenance of, 65; taxable
    income and gains from, 59–60
ventures, manufacturing: earnings from, 61, 61*t*; evaluation of, 61;
    framed antique tiles, 63; quiltmaking example, 47–48, 50–51,
    51–52
ventures, retail: antiques business example, 54–59; clothing accessories
    store example, 135–136, 135*t*, 136*t*; clothing store example,
    108–109; earnings from, 62, 62*t*; evaluation of, 62; framed
    antique tiles, 63; jewelry store example, 87–89

W
wage, base: example, 12–13; hours paid at, 12–13. *see also*
    compensation; rates
wall-hangings (case example): earnings from sales, 81, 82*t*; production
    costs, 76, 76*t*–77*t*, 77–78, 78–79
web sites: Federal government, 64n2, 142–143, 143*t*; general e-
    references, 143, 144*t*; IRS, 64n2, 142–143; small business
    references, 142–143, 142*t*
weekly revenues, example, 86, 86*t*
wholesale prices, 96
Why Knot, Inc. (retail store). *see* retail stores
workers: distinctions between contractors and employees, 74–76; job
    attributes of employees, 75. *see also* contractors; salaried
    professionals or employees
workers, hourly: expected earnings per hour, 21, 22*t*; minimum number
    of hours needed, 33; total compensation for, 23–24, 25*t*–26*t*
workers, part-time: expected earnings per hour worked, 22, 22*t*; hourly
    wage rates for, 16, 16*t*; opportunity cost for, 16–17, 17*t*

Y
Yahoo, 144*t*